The Snowman's Guide to

PERSONAL FINANCE

A simple approach to managing your money

STEVEN ARNOTT

The Snowman's Guide to Personal Finance

ISBN 978-1-7770173-0-9

www.snowmansguide.com

Table of Contents

Introduction

There's only one thing that causes Canadians more stress than our winters. After all, they're frigid, dark and unrelenting. Everyone has a traumatic winter experience to best any story a friend may share. But at the same time, our winters allow for a slew of enjoyable activities. You can skate, sled, drink hot chocolate by the fire or most importantly—as I've now learned—build a snowman.

The answer to the question likely on your mind is personal finance. It's the only thing Canadians consistently find more stressful than winter months—and for many of the same reasons. Student loans, housing affordability and financial illiteracy bring feelings of being restricted, left out in the cold and helpless.

The Challenge

Financial products, like insurance, a mortgage or an investment account, are confusing. There are countless options to choose from and lines of fine print to read. In addition, Canadians continue to borrow more money than ever before and pay higher fees relative to other countries. Selecting the wrong product for your needs can add thousands in additional costs each year. Not taking advantage of certain products altogether can be even worse. You could miss out on hundreds of thousands in growth on your savings or place your family in financial hardship if something terrible were to happen.

While we face unique challenges in Canada, the fact remains that managing money is hard for everyone. As a species, we've only needed to budget our money for the future for a small portion of our existence. Many of the behaviours that served us well in the past make it difficult to take the steps required to be financially successful.

The Solution

While the cards seem to be stacked against us, similarly to our winters, this doesn't have to be the case. Improving your financial literacy will allow you to take advantage of the right products and mindsets to better manage your money. This book provides simple and actionable steps to help you do just that. The best part is that these steps are as rewarding and simple to understand as building a snowman after a fresh snowfall.

Origins of *The Snowman's Guide*

The first idea for this book originated in 2012 after a dinner with my younger brother and a close friend. I was impressed to learn my brother had set aside a handy amount of money from years of saving. However, concern arose as I learned his money was in a chequing account.

Immediately, I mentioned the need to invest for the future to protect his savings from inflation. I tried to explain that each day his money was worth less because things generally become more expensive over time.

In the end, I found success through a simple analogy. I explained that his money in a chequing account was like water in a bucket sitting in the sun. Even though you can't see anything happening, the sun slowly evaporates the water until there's nothing left. Money sitting in a chequing account without earning interest slowly becomes less useful to you. Gradually, the value diminishes until it's effectively gone.

I realized two things at that moment. Fundamentals of personal finance are less widely known than I'd thought, and analogies can bridge the gap between what people know and what they want to learn.

Since that first idea in 2012, I've focused a great deal of my time to help Canadians save and invest their money. I've learned the theories and best practices through thousands of hours of study for school and industry exams. I've also learned practical approaches that Canadians follow through over 10,000 conversations with investors. Through combining theory and practice, this book provides steps that work and explains why.

How to Use This Book

This book is broken into three sections to provide you with the foundation you need to be financially successful. In addition, it's intended to serve as a reference point for the future. Not all topics may be relevant to your current situation, but by learning about them now, you'll be able to use them later.

- Part I outlines saving and investing.
- Part II provides additional tools, like budgeting and account options.
- Part III explains where to go next and what to consider along the way.

The analogy of building a snowman is used throughout the book to provide a consistent framework, tying everything together. This will help you understand and recall these important ideas as they become relevant for your life. If you have questions or feedback as you progress through the book, please let me know at steven@snowmansguide.com.

Part I:
Building a Snowman

Your income is where we'll begin to demonstrate how personal finance is as simple as building a snowman. We'll compare money earned to a fresh snowfall and discuss the similarities in next steps. The section ends with the first analogy I used to help my brother years ago. We'll compare inflation and its impact on your money to a snowman stuck in the blistering sun.

Along the way, we'll cover:

1. Setting aside money as it's earned to pay off debt or to save
2. Investing your savings to help them grow
3. Choosing the right investments for your needs
4. Taking on the right amount of risk to reach your goals
5. Protecting your savings from unexpected expenses

Chapter 1

A Fresh Snowfall:
Your Income

The bell rings to signal the start of recess at a primary school. The students race out of class, excited for the fresh snowfall that's been distracting them all morning. Their focus is simple: to build the best and biggest snowman possible. The fresh, damp snow allows snowballs to be created effortlessly. The unpacked, abundant field ensures the snowman will be large, round and done by the end of recess.

The children are unaware that the steps they're about to take building a snowman are the same they'll eventually take to prepare their financial futures. The reasoning is quite simple. The growth, maintenance and enjoyment of creating a snowman mimics the growth, maintenance and enjoyment of a successful financial plan. This is where we'll draw our first analogy and begin to learn the most important steps within personal finance through building a snowman.

Getting to Your Income First

Think of this fresh snowfall as your paycheque or source of income. Each new paycheque presents a vast field of snow—or money—that you now control. Imagine if the school children hadn't rushed to the fields to build a snowman that recess. Imagine if they had waited days or even weeks before beginning. What the children likely would have found by then isn't a field of opportunity, but instead a field of trampled down snow.

If you wait to set money aside until after it's burned a hole in your pocket, you won't be nearly as successful. Instead, it's best to set it aside the moment you receive it. Be the first to your paycheque to ensure it doesn't get trampled down by other spending.

This demonstrates the importance of setting aside a bit of your income as it's earned. Doing so ensures you're able to take advantage of that field of snow before it gets rundown. After all, just as the seasons change and the snow inevitably disappears, you'll eventually reach a point in your life where you no longer wish or are able to work and must rely on your savings to support you from there.

Income Over Your Lifetime

In addition to using analogies throughout this book, I'll rely heavily on individual examples to make things real and actionable. For our first example, let's consider Kelly, who's starting to save for retirement. Kelly is twenty-five, earning $40,000 a year and wants to retire at age sixty. Setting aside 10% of her income—the equivalent of $333 a month—until retirement would collect $140,000. It's surprising how much money the average person earns and spends in a lifetime without realizing it. At $40,000 a year, Kelly would earn $1.4 million over thirty-five years. If she's not careful, she could have very little left over to show for it.

Small purchases add up over time and can erode a paycheque. Therefore, it's critical to get to your income first and set a portion aside before it's trampled down to nothing.

While not all savings goals are as long-term as retirement, the steps remain the same. Take, for instance, a couple saving for a down payment on a new home. Between them, they earn $95,000 a year and hope to have enough for a down payment in three years. By setting aside 10% of their income—or $13 each per day—for the next three years, the couple would accumulate a total of $28,500. The first step to achieve any financial goal, big or small, is to get to your money before it's been spent and set it aside for the future.

Obstacle: The Temptation to Spend

The issue most people run into when trying to save is the persistent temptation to spend their money. This is due to human nature and our difficulty considering long-term benefits in the face of short-term rewards. It's also what keeps most of us from going to bed on time or tackling that to-do list. We prefer the immediate rewards of doing something else over the long-term gains of getting it done. Therefore, we push the challenge off for another day. It's so hard to save, even though we know we need to, because there's an immediate reward to spending.

The best way to fix this is by automatically transferring your money to another account immediately as it's earned. Keeping your savings out of sight and out of mind is a useful strategy to avoid temptation. The first step is to open a new account with your preferred financial institution—for instance a bank, credit union or digital offering. Once the account has been set up, there are several ways you can transfer over your savings.

Most financial institutions have a service known as a recurring transfer. It's an automatic, scheduled transfer of money from one account to another. This can be used to transfer a portion of your income the day after it's received. For example, if you're paid $1,300 every other Friday, you could schedule a transfer of $150 for every other Saturday. Transferring money before it's spent ensures that saving for the future isn't left to the last minute and potentially forgotten.

If transferring a set amount of money on a regular basis doesn't work for you, there's another option available. Some financial institutions allow you to transfer money from one account to another every time you make a purchase. For instance, as you pay for your $12 dinner, $1 would also be withdrawn and transferred to your savings account. By transferring money whenever you make a purchase, the act of saving becomes less noticeable. You also ensure that money is being saved because to make any purchases, you must also put aside some money for the future.

Obstacle: Thinking You Need the Money Now

Some people postpone setting aside money because they feel it's needed today. You likely have expenses and obligations that your money is earmarked for.

However, what's commonly noticed, and surprisingly so, is that the money you set aside in savings is rarely missed. Quite quickly, most people find their expenses decrease to match the amount of money remaining after savings have been put aside. We tend to spend the money we have available simply because it's there, not because we need to. As a result, setting money aside allows you to save for the future without much of an impact on your current standard of living. To experience it yourself, try setting aside an extra $5 a day and see if you notice. Even that small change would add up to $9,125 over five years. You can start as small as you're comfortable with and gradually increase the amount as your spending habits adjust.

Obstacle: Thinking It's Too Late

Many people worry it's too late to start saving and feel they're too far behind to make a difference. While starting early helps, it's not the only way to reach your goals. You'll be amazed how quickly small changes to savings habits can add up. It's never too late to start putting away money for a car, a down payment on a house or your retirement. Every dollar you put away brings you closer to achieving your financial goals.

Take Darryl for instance, who's forty-five and hasn't started saving for retirement. He's currently making $50,000 a year and is looking to retire at sixty-five. He's decided to set aside 15% of his income for a value of $625 a month. Even with starting at forty-five, Darryl can set aside $150,000 before reaching retirement. Again, this illustrates how regular deposits to a savings account will gradually build to a very useful sum of money.

Budgeting

You can find areas to reduce spending by creating a budget and comparing it to your current expenses. We'll discuss budgeting in further detail in Chapter 6. The main finding is that you can save for the future while maintaining your current standard of living. Through listing and ranking activities that bring you the most satisfaction, you can ensure there's enough money for your top priorities even while setting savings aside.

Paying Off Debt

So far, we've assumed the income you're setting aside is going into a savings account. However, more commonly these days you may benefit from first paying off some loans. We'll cover managing debt in greater detail in Chapter 7. The most important lesson is to pay off high-interest debt before you start setting aside money in a savings account.

High-interest debt generally charges more than 10% interest. It can include credit cards, payday loans and some personal loans. These loans are dangerous because the interest charged means you're constantly fighting an uphill battle. The interest is like gravity dragging you backwards as you try to roll a snowball up a steep incline.

The steps to pay back a loan are the same as setting up your savings. Get to your income first and set aside as much as you comfortably can. Gradually look for ways to lower your spending to make larger payments toward your loan. The key is to pay enough to cover any interest charges and then as much as you can to repay the original loan amount.

Final Thoughts

Whether through conscious or automatic transfers, saving for the future is a necessity. By getting to your money first and setting some aside, you'll be better financially prepared. Just as the children ran for the fresh snowfall, ensure you're getting to your money before it's been trampled.

Key Takeaways

- Get to your money first and set aside savings, so you maintain your standard of living in the future.
- Start today and build your savings habits gradually to avoid taking on too much change at once.
- Automate your savings to remove the temptation to spend.

Chapter 2

The Snowball Effect: Growing Your Savings

Now that you've seen just how quickly regular savings can add up, it's time to discuss the benefits of putting those savings to work. You can invest your savings to earn more money over time. For example, you can deposit your money in a high-interest savings account. Financial institutions pay you cash—called interest—for keeping your money with them. This interest helps grow your savings, allowing you to reach your goals sooner.

Compound Growth

If you leave your money in the account, you'll continue to be paid more interest. You're paid interest both for the money you originally saved and the interest you keep in the account. This process of earning interest on your interest is an example of compound growth. Compound growth—in this case, compound interest—is the most powerful tool available to help you reach your financial goals.

Every month you leave your money in the high-interest savings account, you earn more and more interest. Eventually, the money you set aside combined with the interest leads to a much larger account balance than you'd expect.

Think of a snowball. What starts as a small ball begins to collect additional snow as it's rolled through the field. The snowball grows, and as you continue pushing, it collects snow at a faster and faster rate. The longer you continue, the faster it picks up snow and the larger it becomes. This is the same process your money goes through with compound interest. Your initial savings collect larger and larger amounts of interest, allowing your money to work for you.

Exhibit 1 – A snowball rolling over snow grows at a faster and faster rate.

The growth rate you earn and the length of time you leave your savings invested are critical. The higher the growth rate, the faster compounding works to your advantage. In addition, the longer you invest, the more times your earnings will compound.

Growth Rate

To see the impact of compound growth on your savings, we'll consider three individual cases with different growth rates.

In the first case, we'll consider a $5,000 savings account with 0.5% yearly interest. With such a low interest rate, it will take a while to see substantial growth. In fact, it would take 139 years for the original $5,000 to grow to $10,000. This illustrates why having money sitting around earning low interest rates isn't helping you to build up your savings.

The second case is a savings account with 1.5% yearly interest. At this rate, it's possible to grow the $5,000 into $10,000 in roughly forty-seven years. This means the initial $5,000 in savings has effectively gone to work for forty-seven years and earned an additional $5,000. To think of it another way, you're being paid to do something that is already benefiting you—saving for your future.

Finally, if we consider an annual growth rate of 7%, that initial $5,000 would reach $10,000 in just over ten years.

Exhibit 2 – It could either take 139 years or ten years to double your money, depending on if you're earning 0.5% or 7% a year.

Annual Growth Rate	0.5%	1.5%	3%	5%	7%
Years to Double Your Money	139	47	24	14	10

A 7% growth rate will continue to allow the $10,000 to grow into $20,000 ten years later and $40,000 in an additional ten years.

Exhibit 3 – Similarly to the rolling snowball in Exhibit 1, compound growth has a powerful impact on the size of your savings over time.

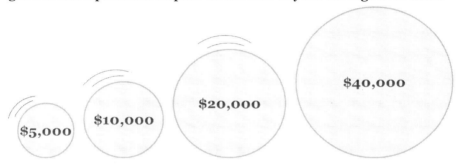

Finally, we'll compare how two growth rates that appear similar at first glance—7% and 8%—will grow over thirty-five years. With an initial $10,000 growing at 7% a year, you'd have $106,800 after thirty-five years. While this is exceptional growth that would help you reach your goal, let's consider the second rate. If you achieved 8% yearly growth, your $10,000 would grow to $147,900 over the same thirty-five-year timeframe. Even though the difference in rates is only 1%, you stand to earn over 40% more.

Length of Time

The sooner you start saving for the future, the longer your money can grow. The benefit of increased time can be seen with an example. Let's watch two new grads, Daniel and Craig, as they begin their professional lives. Daniel realizes the importance of setting aside savings, and for the first ten years after college, he saves $5,000 a year. From age twenty-three through thirty-two, Daniel sets aside a total of $50,000. If he allows that money to grow at 7% a year, at age sixty, Daniel would have a total of $459,300. Because Daniel started so early, the deposits he made grew to nearly ten times what he put aside.

Craig has heard stories of building personal wealth but has other priorities after graduation. It's because of this that he postpones saving until the age of forty. To reach $459,300 in savings by the time Craig is sixty, he'd need to deposit $11,200 a year for twenty years. This would result in Craig setting aside $224,000 compared to Daniel's $50,000. By delaying his savings by eighteen years, Craig didn't allow his money the same opportunity to grow that Daniel's had. By starting to save—even small amounts—as soon as you can, you'll allow your savings the most time possible to benefit from compound growth.

Exhibit 4 – After setting $5,000 aside for the first ten years after graduation, Daniel was able to sit back and watch his savings grow. Meanwhile, due to the shortened timeline Craig gave his money, he had to set aside $11,200 a year for twenty years to catch up.

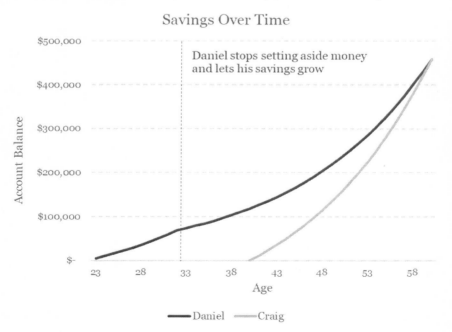

Savings Over Time

Exhibit 5 – Presented in a different way, Craig had to contribute over four times what Daniel did to arrive at the same account balance at the age of sixty.

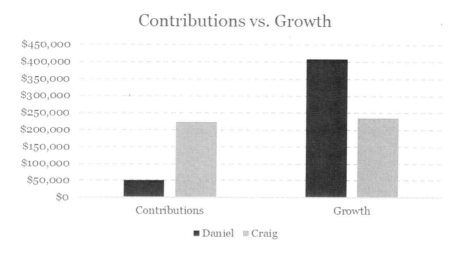

Examples from Chapter 1

In the previous chapter, we considered three examples of saving for the future. Kelly was starting early to save for retirement, a couple planned to buy a house in three years and Darryl was eager to catch up on his retirement goal. These examples showed that with regular deposits to a savings account, you can amass a great deal of money. Let's revisit those examples and consider compounded returns on the savings.

In our first example, Kelly set aside $4,000 a year for thirty-five years. As a result, we determined she'd save $140,000. If she were able to earn a 7% yearly growth rate, the balance would reach a value of $553,000—nearly four times the savings without growth.

In our second example, the couple set aside $9,500 a year for three years for a down payment, resulting in $28,500. Even with only a short period for the money to grow, the couple would have $30,500 if they earned a 7% annual return.

Finally, Darryl set aside $7,500 a year for a period of twenty years and saved $150,000 toward retirement. If he earned 7% annually, he would have $307,500—more than double the amount that was set aside.

Exhibit 6 – Kelly and Darryl earned more from growth than either set aside themselves. In fact, Kelly only set aside 25% of what she ended up with.

Saver	Per year	Years	Saved	Growth	Total
Kelly	$ 4,000	35	$ 140,000	**$ 413,000**	$ 553,000
Couple	$ 9,500	3	$ 28,500	**$ 2,000**	$ 30,500
Darryl	$ 7,500	20	$ 150,000	**$ 157,500**	$ 307,500

What you're witnessing is money hard at work making the most of compound growth. By placing savings in an account with interest—or any return—the money you've saved earns you additional income as the years go by. The growth accumulates and shortens the time needed to reach your financial goals.

Final Thoughts

Compound growth is a tremendous tool available to those who choose to use it. It's been used before by children in the field building a snowman, and now it's time you put it to use to build your savings. By starting early and earning returns, you can put your money to work saving for your goals.

Key Takeaways

- Invest your savings to earn interest or other returns and put your money to work.
- Compound growth is critical to reaching your long-term financial goals.
- Earning a higher growth rate and starting early are key to growing your savings.

Chapter 3

Packing Snow:
Quality of Investments

Last chapter we saw that the growth rate earned on your savings has a huge impact on your financial success. A natural question that may come to mind is how to earn the highest growth rate possible on your savings. While the rate of return is important for your financial well-being, so is the quality of your investments.

It's common knowledge that different types of snow are better or worse at keeping a snowman packed together. The first thing most people want to know before starting to build a snowman is whether the snow is "packing snow". The depth and freshness of a snowfall has little value if the quality of the snow isn't right. The remainder of this chapter will discuss steps to ensure your investments are the equivalent of packing snow and not simply fluff.

The investment options that we'll cover in depth in part II of this book include:

- Stocks – Chapter 12
- Guaranteed investment certificates (GICs) – Chapter 13
- Bonds – Chapter 13
- Mutual funds – Chapter 14
- Exchange-traded funds (ETFs) – Chapter 14
- Real estate – Chapter 15

These investments offer differing rates of return. The rate of return may be known upfront when you invest, or unknown until later. In addition to these, we've already discussed one of the most versatile and widely used investment products, a high-interest savings account.

The Two Main Investment Types

When it comes to investment options, there are enough complicated choices to make anyone's head spin. Many of the products were created for investors with complex needs and elaborate opinions on what the future holds. The great news is that most of the opportunity is found in two simple investment types. You can purchase ownership, or you can lend your money.

Exhibit 7 – Investing is as simple as owning or lending. You can purchase something, like real estate, and own it. Or you can temporarily lend your money and receive it back, plus interest, sometime in the future.

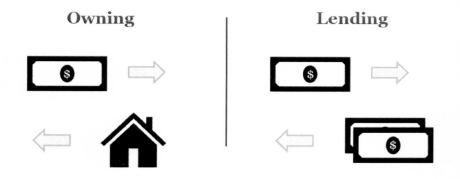

| Owning | Lending |

You don't need to know everything about all the options we'll discuss to start benefiting from investing. What is crucial, however, is that with any investment choice you make, you put in the time to learn what risks you're exposing your hard-earned money to.

Personal research and the assistance of educated professionals— such as a financial advisor—will expose you to the options available. Some products you'll come across are great investments, the type of investment that could easily be compared to packing snow. However, there are some out there that, either by creation or misuse, can be very damaging to your savings.

Red Flags

A major red flag is any investment that seems too good to be true. Because of the number of educated people constantly watching for a free lunch, it's unlikely for a sure thing to go overlooked.

An investment that claims equal risk to another and yet offers twice the return is cause for skepticism. Some products deduct a portion of the investment for fees, either when you deposit or withdraw. Another potential cause for concern is small print that places conditions on returns. In the worst of cases, it's possible the investment could be fraudulent altogether, causing the loss of savings. Before investing, be sure to learn about the rules and check the credibility of the institution offering the investment.

Forecasting Investment Performance

Now that you know some of the dangers to watch for when searching through investments, you're left with a range of great choices for your money. As we mentioned previously, some investments offer a known growth rate up front. An example is a high-interest savings account that offers 2% interest per year. Other investments, like stocks and real estate, are uncertain. This is because they depend on how much you're able to sell them for in the future.

As you compare investment options, one thing to consider is how they've performed in the past. While it's no guarantee of what you'll earn, it can give you an idea and help with your decision. For example, the Canadian stock market grew at an average annual rate of 7% over the past twenty years. And over any given ten years, the return ranged from an average of 3% to 11%.

Long-Term Investing

In the last chapter, we mentioned that starting early was important to allow your money time to compound. Another reason to invest with a long timeframe is to minimize the uncertainty some investments hold. To demonstrate, let's consider if you had invested in the Canadian stock market sometime in the last two decades. If you were invested for only a single year, you could have lost as much as 42% or made as much as 61%. In 2002, as the tech bubble burst, the Canadian stock market lost roughly 14%. In 2008, the recession led to a decline of 33%. On the other hand, the recoveries in 2003 and 2009 led to returns of 25% and 34%.

However, if you were invested for ten years, your average annual return would have ranged between 3% to 11%. Therefore, even though some investments are uncertain, the return is more predictable over longer periods.

Exhibit 8 – The year-to-year growth rate of most investments is unpredictable and can vary significantly. For instance, over one year, you could lose or gain a large percentage of your savings. However, returns over longer periods are more predictable.

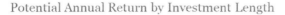

Potential Annual Return by Investment Length

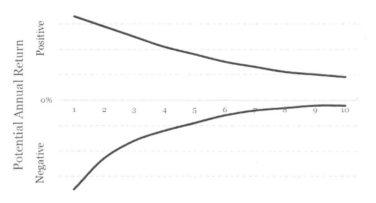

Number of Years Invested

Investing over a long period of time requires two things. Your goal must be far enough away, and you must have the emotional strength to avoid selling your investments before you need to.

The first point is a simple decision. For short-term savings where you need most of your money within the next year or two—like a vacation or car—it's dangerous to invest in unpredictable options, like the stock market or real estate. However, if it's a long-term savings goal—like retirement—then these investment options are more suitable.

The second point may not seem like it now, but it's arguably the most challenging part of investing. You must ignore the constant ups and downs your investments will go through and remember the long-term potential the investment holds.

To give you strength for the inevitable day your investments go down in value, consider your reaction to a warm day in winter. If midway through January the temperature increased above freezing, you wouldn't pack your winter jacket in a box and drive out to your storage locker to put it away for the year. You'd know that while it may be warm today, or even for the next week, winter always has a way of returning when you least expect it.

Investments, as we've mentioned, go up and down as good and bad news come to pass. It's possible that at the end of a year's worth of investing your savings may not have grown at all, or they could have lost money. If you panic at the sight of losses and sell your investments, you'll no longer be exposed to the great potential they hold. Yes, investments lose money from time to time, but that's the nature of the unknown. However, as has been shown throughout history, successful investments outweigh the ones that fail. As a result, on a long-term basis, you're likely to experience the growth you require to reach your goals, provided you give your investments enough time.

Another thing that can challenge you emotionally, even when your investments are growing, is someone saying you should sell. Whether it's a friend or a financial analyst on TV, there's never a shortage of people claiming to know what's coming next.

The first thing we need to agree on is that no one knows for sure what the future holds. Instead, people rely on historical trends and probabilities of what could happen in the future. Based on this, financial analysts and TV personalities make predictions about where investments will go next.

The approach these people follow is quite like forecasting the weather. You may have realized over the years that weather forecasts are rarely exact. They may be close some days or get the temperature correct the next, but the consistency is unpredictable. It's not due to a lack of effort but, instead, to the challenge of predicting something with so many random variables involved. Therefore, when you hear that the market has reached its peak and that you should sell, think back to the last time a major snowfall caught you off guard and forecasts had read a 0% chance of snow, and remind yourself no one knows what the future holds.

Diversifying Your Investments

As we've now covered, many investments offer unpredictable returns. 2000 was a great year to own tech stocks, and the next year wasn't. Similarly, 2005 was a great time to be invested in real estate, and 2008 wasn't. A second way to make investing more predictable is to have a wide range of investments. This approach, referred to as diversification, is another key tool available to help you reach your financial goals.

For example, instead of investing all your money in the Canadian stock market, you can invest in different geographies and investment options. The advantage to this approach is that not all investments behave the same each year. Canadian oil companies may fall by 10% the same year that European bonds increase by 6%. By holding both Canadian oil stocks and European bonds, your total savings would grow at a more predictable rate.

Exhibit 9 – The following three individual investments offer varying growth each year. If a large portion of your money is in a single investment, your returns will be more irregular.

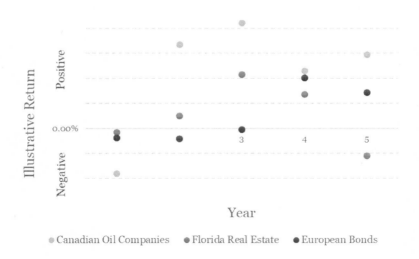

Illustrative Investment Returns

Exhibit 10 – Investing your money equally in all three of the above investments smooths out your returns and reduces uncertainty.

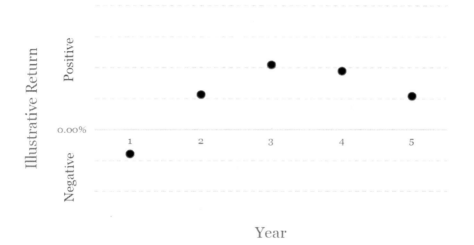

Illustrative Returns With Diversification

You could guess—or speculate—which investment will outperform the others. However, by diversifying the number and type of investments, you'll minimize the risk of major losses.

Let's explore another snowman analogy to help solidify the importance of diversification in reaching your financial goals. While individual days throughout the winter may call for large snowfalls and others for none, we know with near certainty that there will be snow during the winter. You could try to pick individual days that will bring in the best results, but if you look at the whole season rather than any small part, there's much less risk you'll be wrong.

If you were tasked with building as many snowmen as you could in a winter, there's several ways you could do it. You could watch the weather report and decide on a few days with high forecasted snowfall. Or you could choose to set aside a little of your time every day to take advantage of any fresh powder that may fall.

The first option is like picking individual investments and hoping that they're better than all the rest. While it's possible the forecasts are right, if they're not, you'll build zero snowmen all winter.

The second option is like diversifying your investments. Since it's so hard to predict which single day will bring the most packing snow, you can spread your time across the whole season, ensuring that a few days will allow you a chance to build a snowman.

Final Thoughts

This chapter isn't meant to frighten you away from investing. It's designed to inform you of the risks and uncertainties involved and provide several key steps to address them. Investing doesn't have to be complicated and time-consuming. Take on as much as you're comfortable with and seek guidance from others as required.

Key Takeaways

- Create a list of investment options you understand and trust.
- Spread your money across a diverse assortment of investment options.
- Give your investments time, allowing them the best chance to grow.

Chapter 4

Rolling Choices:
Risk and Reward

The previous chapter included the words "uncertain," "unknown" and "unpredictable" a combined total of eleven times. While the wording varied, the message remained constant. One of the most central ideas when investing is the uncertainty of what will happen in the future.

Defining Risk

Some investments fail. Companies compete to address the same need of the same client, and in most cases, only one can win. One business is built assuming the future will look a certain way, and another is built assuming it won't. As a result, investments fluctuate in value as the uncertain world ahead comes into better focus. If the future that benefits your investments doesn't happen, there's a risk that you could lose money.

Ultimately, what matters to you as an investor is whether you reach your goal or not. For example, you may have a goal to save $30,000 in three years for a down payment on a house. If you set aside $10,000 each year for the next three years into a savings account, you know with certainty that you'll reach your goal. There's no risk your investment will decrease in value and that you'll miss your goal. If, however, you invest the $10,000 each year in stocks, you face the risk of losing money and not having enough for your down payment.

Exhibit 11 – Uncertainty results in a risk that some investments will lose money. If you lose money, you may not achieve your goal.

Uncertainty   Risk of Loss   Risk of Missing Goal

A   B

Different investments carry different levels of risk. Often, they're separated into two categories of low risk and high risk.

Low-Risk Investments

An example of a low-risk investment is a savings account at a bank. The chance that the bank won't have the exact amount of money that you expect when you withdraw is extremely low. Because the interest rate is known and the bank guarantees your deposit, you're assured that when it comes time to take out your money, you'll have what you expected.

High-Risk Investments

An example of a high-risk investment is buying a stock. When you buy a stock, you receive ownership of a portion of a business. Over time, the business earns money, releases products and gains or loses customers. As a result, the value of your portion of the business fluctuates up and down with good and bad news. Because the future value of that stock is unknown, there's a risk that when you sell it, you won't receive enough money for your goal.

We'll cover the stock market further in Chapter 12. To summarize, your stock can increase or decrease in value over time with no guarantee of your initial savings. If you pay $20 for a stock and over five years the company does well, your investment may be worth $40. However, if the company struggles, the stock may only be worth $10. The factors that determine how these investments perform are mostly unpredictable, which is why there's a higher level of risk.

Accepting Risk for a Reward

Very few people enjoy taking on risk for the fun of it. If there's a chance an investment will fail, then there needs to be a significant payoff if it does work out. Otherwise, you're better off investing in something with a more predictable future. Therefore, riskier investments demand a higher return.

To illustrate, savings accounts that have very little risk offer low interest rates relative to other options. If you're willing to take on more risk and lend your money to a company or government, you can earn a higher interest rate. And if you're comfortable with the risk of buying stocks, you have the potential to earn even higher returns.

Exhibit 12 – To incentivize you to take on more risk, investments must offer additional reward in the form of higher average returns.

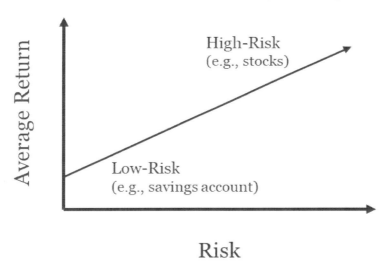

In Chapter 2, we saw that compound growth, especially through higher growth rates, is critical to achieving your goals. Riskier investments, like stocks, are one way people have historically earned these higher growth rates.

Risk and Reward When Building a Snowman

When you're building a snowman, the primary risk is that you don't finish in time. This could be caused by a snowball cracking or crumpling.

In a backyard or field, there are plenty of ways to work with friends and family to build a snowman. Each option has pros and cons and will differ in how quickly you reach your goal.

For example, wouldn't it be great to push a snowball down a steep hill, allowing gravity to do all the work? As the snowball accelerates and picks up more and more snow, it would be hard not to grin with satisfaction. But this approach could end in sorrow if the snowball were to split in half on a hard bounce or collision with a tree. This is where the trade-off between risk and reward comes in. While the reward of successfully rolling the snowball down the hill is substantial, it also carries significant risk.

The decisions required to grow your savings are like the options available when building a snowman. There's an option to take a less risky path and grow your savings slow and steady over time. Or, through taking on additional risk, there's an opportunity to grow your savings at a faster rate. As we'll see shortly, there are several important things to consider as you decide whether to take on risk to help you grow your savings.

Managing Risk

As we saw in the last chapter, the closer you are to needing your money, the more dangerous risky investments are. If your investments suddenly decline in value, it could leave you vulnerable. The little time remaining may not be enough for your investments to grow back to the amount you need. While risk becomes less desirable as you near your goal, we've seen that earning higher returns is important. Since low-risk investments don't offer the returns required to take full advantage of compound growth, it's common to invest in some high-risk investments.

One strategy is to accept higher risk when there's plenty of time for your money to recover from any decline in value. While most investments carry risk, the amount decreases the longer the investment is held. Historically, the longer the investment period, the lower the chance of a loss. Therefore, many people invest in riskier investments early in the savings process and gradually switch to less risky investments as the need for the money approaches.

A Tale of Two Snowmen

To demonstrate why it's important to consider your timeframe when deciding to take on risk, let's consider two instances of building a snowman.

The first is a group of children with only a single recess left before Christmas break. By the end of the thirty minutes, they hope to have a snowman built to show visiting relatives. The children will likely be quite careful with their actions and may favour a smaller, more stable snowman. They'll want to be sure nothing goes wrong with such limited time left. These children are in a similar situation to someone investing for a short period of time. For example, if you have a vacation planned in six months, there's little time available to recover your money if a riskier investment decreased in value.

The second group of children we'll consider has an entire weekend free of chores and homework. Their hope is to build a snowman that's the envy of the neighbourhood. They experiment with rolling techniques, knowing full well some will fail. They stack snowballs precariously on top of each other in hopes they'll stand tall. Their reasoning is quite simple. Through accepting higher risk, they stand a better chance of creating a snowman the size of which they've never seen. After all, with a great deal of time to recover from cracked or fallen snowballs, they'd be wasting potential opportunities by sticking to a safe and standard build.

Gradually Lowering Your Risk

The second group of children start with a full weekend ahead and a willingness to accept higher risk. However, as they work through Saturday and early Sunday, they gradually take on less risk in their tactics. The simple reason is that if the snowman fell over on Sunday afternoon, they'd have little time to recover before bedtime.

To demonstrate how this transition works with your investments, we'll use a brief example. Let's consider a recent college graduate named Katelyn, who's twenty-two years old. Her retirement is so far off she likely hasn't even started thinking about what it will entail. However, with such a long time period, any savings she puts toward retirement will have the chance to recover from an initial decline in value. Because of this long timeframe, Katelyn may find it's best to put most of her retirement savings in higher-risk, higher-return investments.

A split of 90% high risk and 10% low risk could allow her savings to grow at a faster rate in the early years. As time passes and retirement approaches, the amount of risk she desires will begin to decrease. At age thirty-five, she may determine that 75% in high-risk and 25% in low-risk investments is more comfortable. Once Katelyn reaches the age of sixty, she'll likely find a more conservative split of 50% high risk and 50% low risk to be most appropriate. This trend toward lower-risk, or more stable, investments continues as her need for the money approaches.

Exhibit 13 – Katelyn gradually reduces the percent of her high-risk investments, preferring low-risk investments as the need for her savings approaches.

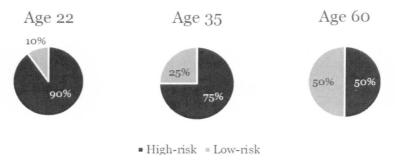

The Right Level of Risk

The first step to managing risk—described through Katelyn's story above—is to make a choice about your ability to handle risk given the time remaining to your goal. Another consideration mentioned in the last chapter is your emotional comfort with risk. If losing money could cause you distress and potentially cause you to sell your investments, then a lower level of risk may be appropriate.

You may become more comfortable over time as you experience the ups and downs of investing and see the power of higher returns.

Maintaining Your Target Risk

Once you've determined your starting level of risk, the next step is to check in on your investments from time to time. As we've discussed, low- and high-risk investments offer differing returns and differing levels of certainty. As a result, one type of investment may outperform the other and grow at a faster rate over time. If this happens, your starting level of risk can stray off track. If your high-risk investments perform very well, what started as 70% of your money in high-risk investments may end up being 75%. Throughout time, often annually, there's a need to check your investments to ensure you're still at the level of risk you intended.

Exhibit 14 – Your target risk exposure was chosen for a reason. Therefore, if your investments stray from your target, it's common to rebalance your investments from time to time.

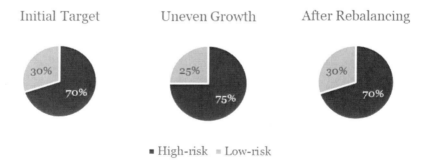

This idea of increased growth on only a portion of your investments can also be illustrated in the rolling of a snowball. You start with a round ball of snow. While it rolls through the snow, it doesn't always grow evenly. The snowball can become disfigured as it collects too much snow on one side or the other. The steps taken to address the inconsistent growth of a snowball are the same as you'd take with your investments. Periodically, you stop, take a moment, smooth out or rotate your uneven snowball and begin again from a balanced state. This process minimizes the chance of a piece breaking off unexpectedly due to its exposed state.

Final Thoughts

You've now seen why investments that provide higher returns, which are so crucial in growing your savings, carry higher risk. This risk becomes less attractive as you approach a need for your money. After setting your target risk level, there's a need to rebalance your investments if you're off track. These simple steps will help you to increase your returns without taking on more risk than you can handle.

Key Takeaways

- Some investments will lose money, potentially placing your goal at risk.
- Taking on some risk is required to earn higher returns, which are vital for growing your money.
- To manage this trade-off, accept a suitable amount of risk and gradually lower it as your goal approaches.

Chapter 5

Evaporation and Rainfall:
Inflation and Unexpected Expenses

Weather can take a significant toll on a snowman's longevity. Both the beating rays of the sun and the wear of drizzling rainfall can quickly shrink a snowman's stature. The sun heats up the surface of the snowman, causing layers of glistening snow to slowly evaporate. The rainfall also heats up the snowman and drags bits of the exterior down to the snowy ground below. In both cases, there are ties that can be made between the well-being of a snowman and your savings.

Inflation

The evaporation caused by the sun's unwavering heat causes the snowman to slowly shrink. A similar effect exists in personal finance, and it has the same results on the value of your savings. The term is inflation, and it means that year by year, the price you pay for the same goods and services increases. In other words, those fables of ten-cent ice cream cones and five-cent bags of candy you may have heard are in fact entirely true. Over time, prices increase, and the value of a loonie slowly shrinks.

Up until now, we've stressed the importance of getting to your money first and setting it aside for future expenses. We've also covered the risk and opportunity of investing your money to help it grow. But one very important and often overlooked component of savings is preparing for inflation. Let's consider two cases to get an idea of how inflation works before continuing.

The Impact of Inflation

The first example of how inflation can impact your savings is an individual buying a new car. An eighteen-year-old walks into a dealership and finds his dream car with a price tag of $27,000. The teenager diligently sets aside money for five years and, on his twenty-third birthday, marches into the dealership with $27,000 in his account. To the young man's horror, as he approaches the new car glistening in the sunlight, there's an unfamiliar tag across its front windshield. The price of the car he's been saving five years for is no longer $27,000 but instead $30,000. Over the past five years due to inflation, the cost of the same model car has increased by $3,000. Therefore, the savings he was able to set aside are unfortunately not enough.

While failing to account for inflation on your dream car would be heartbreaking, the impact is far greater when saving for a long-term goal, like retirement. Our next example is a couple that earns $85,000 a year after tax. They live quite comfortably while setting aside 15% for retirement and 10% for a down payment on a house. With the savings set aside, the couple can live happily off $63,750. It may stand to reason that the couple should be able to live off this same amount each year for the remainder of their lives. However, due to inflation, this isn't the case.

The cost of paying for gas, buying groceries and all other expenses increases over time. The same goods and services the couple can buy with $63,750 today might cost closer to $127,500 when they retire in thirty-five years. If the couple only sets aside enough to spend $63,750 a year in their retirement, their standard of living would drastically decrease after cutting expenses to stay on budget.

Rate of Inflation

The average rate of inflation in Canada has been roughly 2% a year over the last forty years. While there's no guarantee that individual expenses will follow this rate of inflation exactly, on average, the rate has been quite consistent. By planning for inflation on future expenses, you'll ensure you have the money required to make the purchase.

Inflation is another reason why it's very important that you're putting your savings to work by earning a return. Money not earning a return by sitting in a chequing account decreases in value over time, like a snowman left out in the blazing sun.

Unexpected Expenses

With the beating sun accounted for, the second danger to a snowman is rainfall. If left uncovered in the rain, a snowman begins to melt away and once again shrinks in size. The equivalent to rainfall for your savings is an unexpected expense or loss of income. To protect yourself, it's important to put savings aside in a separate account known as a "rainy day"—or emergency—fund.

As we previously saw, a critical step with high-risk investments is ensuring there's enough time before you need the money. If you need to sell an investment early, it could result in large losses or additional fees. Because of this, it's common to develop a buffer zone between unexpected events and your investments.

A Rainy Day Fund

To establish this buffer, it's common to set aside enough money to cover your expenses for three to six months. It's important to do this before starting to save for additional goals in case anything unexpected comes up. If your critical monthly expenses are $2,000, then it's helpful to set aside between $6,000 and $12,000 before beginning to invest toward other goals.

The amount required depends on your current job security, the flexibility of your expenses and any insurance coverage you have. The more exposure you have to the damaging effects of lost income or unexpected expenses, the larger the buffer zone should be. Having readily available money for emergency situations is sure to bring peace of mind.

If you experienced a large expense or job loss without a rainy day fund, it wouldn't be long before you'd be forced to sell your investments to pay for expenses. This could result in losses on what you're selling. The rushed need to sell puts you at the mercy of what someone else will pay. By maintaining a rainy day fund, you can allow your investments the long timeframe they need.

Final Thoughts

As Canadians are aware, the elements can be harsh. While we're most familiar with the challenges of cold, dark winters, we've now seen that rainfall and the sun's beating rays can be equally menacing. It's important to invest your money to offset the effects of inflation. In addition, setting up a rainy day fund will help with any unexpected events and allow you to save for your main goals with peace of mind.

Key Takeaways

- Your future goals will be more expensive than today due to inflation.
- It's important to invest your money, so it's not losing its value over time.
- Set up a rainy day fund with three to six months' expenses to protect your other investments.

Summary I

You've now seen that managing your personal finances is as simple as building a snowman. To help solidify the learnings in part I, the following table outlines the analogies used and the takeaway for each.

Building a Snowman	Personal Finance	Takeaway
Fresh snowfall	Receiving money	Set aside money as it's earned to maximize your chance of success
Rolling uphill	High-interest loans	Pay off high-interest loans first to remove the ongoing interest cost from your expenses
The snowball effect	Compound growth	Put your money to work by earning returns on your savings and allowing them to continue to grow
Packing snow	Investment quality	Screen your investments and diversify across multiple options over a long period of time
Weather forecasts	Analyst expectations	Ignore the noise of analysts that claim the market will go up or down
A split snowball	Shortfall risk	Take an appropriate amount of risk to minimize the chance you fall short of your goal
Rounding out a snowball	Rebalancing	Rebalance your investments to maintain your target amount of risk
Evaporation	Inflation	Earn a return on your savings so you can pay for higher expenses in the future
Rainfall	Unexpected expenses	Prepare for unexpected expenses through setting aside money in a "rainy day" fund

Many of the steps required to set yourself up for success are included above. To make it even simpler to work through, the following list places these steps in sequence.

1. Set aside money as it's earned.
   - ☐ Find what works for you, with a target of 20% across your goals.
   - ☐ Automate this through transfers into a new account.

2. Pay off any high-interest debt.
3. Set up a rainy day fund.
   - ☐ Ensure you're earning interest on the money.
   - ☐ Deposit three to six months' expenses.
4. Invest your money for future goals.
   - ☐ Find the right amount of risk for you and your goals.
   - ☐ Diversify your investments.
5. Stick to your plan and ignore the noise.

A financial plan doesn't need to be complicated and lengthy. Begin where you feel comfortable, and as you learn more and it becomes easier, you can expand your plan. Developing strong savings habits doesn't happen overnight, but the more you practice and consider your future financial needs, the easier it gets.

You now have the foundations of personal finance required to move on to the next part of this book. With tools like compound growth and diversification, your financial goals aren't as far off as they may have initially seemed. In part II, we'll cover additional tools, including budgets, insurance and accounts to lower your taxes. We'll also expand on some of the ideas we mentioned in part I, such as paying off debt and investing in the stock market, fixed income and real estate.

Part II:
The Accessories

As you finish building a snowman, accessories are traditionally added to help encapsulate the joy of the season. Accessories can range from a pair of twigs to a black top hat. Whether they're small or large, simple or fancy, the effect is typically the same. The snowman evolves to a higher, more respectable form. Either way, the snowman serves its purpose, but the use of accessories undeniably improves the result.

The next part of this book will expand on the ideas we've covered so far and introduce new tools. These lessons, like accessories added to a snowman, will enhance your financial plan. This will allow you to take advantage of every available resource, making your job easier as you go. Topics will range from alternate ways of thinking to steps to lower your taxes. You may be able to use some of them starting today, while others may be useful later as your needs change.

To help unify the material we've covered so far with what's to come, simply keep in mind the following three themes.

1. Set money aside for the future.
2. Earn the highest returns possible given the situation.
3. Protect against the threat of the unexpected.

While personal finance may seem wide ranging and complex, most topics help you achieve the above goals. There are ways to lower your expenses or increase your income, allowing you to set aside additional savings. Different investment strategies and tax saving accounts allow you to maximize the return earned on your savings. Insurance and a will can protect your savings from financial risks of the unexpected.

If you can't apply the following chapters to your current situation, it's still worth having a base understanding, so you know when they apply later. This way, you'll avoid missing out on their benefits. For chapters that don't immediately apply, review as much as you can and come back for the specifics when needed. A common approach with financial literacy is to combine a base understanding today with a follow-up review when you need it.

Chapter 6

Expenses and Budgeting

In Chapter 1, we introduced one of the most common challenges people have when trying to save. It's the feeling that you don't earn enough today to set aside money for the future. To address this concern, you could increase the amount of money you're making. This can be done through working a second job, receiving a raise or completing freelance work. Efforts to increase your income can be very helpful to your financial success. There are resources available from free online courses to guides on how to ask for a raise. You can also offer freelance services through a range of communities.

However, you'll likely find that as your income increases, your expenses do as well, leaving you back where you started. There's a natural tendency to spend what you have available, which inflates expenses above what they need to be. If you have $5 for lunch, it's typically possible to find a meal to meet your needs. But if you have $10 to purchase lunch, you'd likely not visit the same spot for a $5 meal.

The tendency to spend more as money becomes available is a large reason why many of us have trouble saving. While rewarding yourself for hard work is encouraged, it's important to do so only after setting aside enough for the future.

In addition to working on your income, a more immediate and often effective option is to focus on what you spend. To demonstrate, let's consider several ways you can rethink your expenses to help you spend less.

Pay Yourself for Spending Wisely

Imagine you're going for dinner with a full wallet and an empty stomach. As you glance down the menu, you see lots of options at different prices. Once you've decided the most you're willing to spend, step back and think about the situation with a different mindset.

Consider the difference between the most you're willing to spend and the cost of the items on the menu. View it as the amount you'll get paid to choose that item. For instance, if the most you're willing to spend is $20 and a cheeseburger costs $14, the price difference of $6 is how much you can be paid to eat. By choosing the cheeseburger, you've saved $6 from what you had previously considered spending. It's a perfect example of a dollar saved being a dollar earned.

Exhibit 15 – Rather than simply looking at the price of menu options, reframe the list and pay yourself while eating.

Standard Menu		Reframed Menu
Entrees		Entrees
Cheeseburger $14		Get paid $6 to eat a cheeseburger
Pizza $17		Get paid $3 to eat a pizza
Ribs $20		Get paid nothing to eat ribs

Receiving an immediate financial reward for wise spending is sometimes enough to sway your mind in the more economical direction. It's hard to turn down ribs if the benefit is so far off, for instance a better retirement. By moving the reward to be in the same timeframe as the ribs, it's easier for your mind to make a fair trade-off. The decision becomes, "Would you rather eat a rack of ribs, or be paid $6 to eat a cheeseburger?"

The simple reframing described above may be enough to change your spending habits. If it's not, you can take the approach one step further. When you make the wise choice to spend less, transfer the difference from your chequing account to your savings account of choice. The tangible reward of seeing the impact of your decision should help you stick to your savings plan.

The High Cost of Convenience

Another way of thinking about expenses is to consider how much you're paying for an hour of convenience. As an example, if you pay $5 to save fifteen minutes picking up a meal, you're paying $20 an hour for your convenience. We often pay for services we can perform or products we can make without realizing how expensive it is. Some expenses are worth paying for, but others may be a bit harder to justify. If it costs you more to do it yourself, or you can better spend your time, then you should likely pay for the service. However, if it's reasonable to do it yourself, then consider avoiding the expense.

Taking a taxi or ride-hailing service instead of public transit could cost you an extra $10 to save twenty minutes. Provided you're not in a rush, it may be worth saving the equivalent of $30 an hour by taking public transit. Instead of treating expenses as necessities that often inflate with your income, look for where it makes sense to cut back. To think of it once again from the income perspective, you're being paid to modify your spending habits.

Spending Your Time

A similar approach is to look at an expense as the number of hours you need to work to pay for it. If you earn $20 an hour, then the cost of purchasing a $40 shirt is comparable to working two hours. By taking the dollar value out of the picture, you can make your decision based on the actual trade-off. In the above example, you're exchanging two hours of work for a new shirt.

Alternatives for Your Money

The final approach we'll discuss is to consider alternatives for your money. Before making a purchase, briefly ask if there's something else more deserving of that money. By getting the highest value out of your spending, you can lower your expenses without sacrificing your standard of living. It's with this idea of getting the most from your money that we'll move on to the topic of budgeting.

Budgeting: What It Is and Isn't

One very important step in managing your spending is creating a budget. Before we discuss how to create a budget and what it should do, let's briefly talk about what it shouldn't do. A good budget shouldn't lower your quality of life through constant guilt and pressure. It shouldn't make you feel like you can't afford to enjoy yourself when the opportunity arises. Instead, a good budget will allow you to spend guilt-free on what's most important to you.

To understand the value of a budget, we need to agree on two facts. First, regardless what your income is, there's a limit to the amount of money you can spend. Second, you have unique preferences and priorities that determine how you live your life. With these two facts in mind, a good budget will maximize the value you get from spending your money.

Let's continue with the idea of making the most of your money and discuss the design of a successful budget. There are things in your life you can't go without. For most, this includes a roof over your head and meals throughout the day. Regardless of what's critical to your life, it's important there's always money available for them. A budget is meant to take your money and assign it dollar by dollar from top to bottom on your list of priorities. Recognizing a budget this way makes it a lot more attractive because you're not saying no to this and no to that, but rather you're saying yes to the things that are most important to you.

Not budgeting doesn't mean you can spend your money on whatever you want because budget or no budget, at the end of the day when the money is gone, there's no more to spend. With a well-planned budget, however, you'll know you got the most from what you had available.

How to Create a Budget

Now that you've seen the importance of a budget and what its goals are, let's discuss the steps to create one.

1. Calculate your income after subtracting taxes and savings.
   - Subtract your savings right away to ensure you get to your money first—as we discussed in Chapter 1.

2. List the items that bring you the most value for your money.
   - This could include rent, groceries, transportation, clothing, meals out, entertainment and many more.
3. Split your income in Step 1 across the items in Step 2.
   - Start with the most important and work your way down.

If you don't have enough for an item on the list, then consider reducing spending elsewhere. The intention is to spend money where you're getting the most value. Your expenses may be too high given your current income level, making it tough to include everything on the list.

The items on your list can be categorized as a required expense, discretionary expense or savings. Below are several examples of how to classify line items and a baseline of how much to spend on each category.

- **Required expenses**, for example housing, groceries and transportation, should be less than 50% of your after-tax income.
- **Discretionary expenses**, for example hobbies, travel and dining out, should be less than 30%.
- **Savings**, for example retirement and loan repayment, should be roughly 20%.

As with any rule of thumb, the percentages are flexible depending on your unique circumstances and priorities. Through shifting around your spending, your ideal budget starts to form. You have now taken a set amount of money and made sure that every dollar will be used to bring you the most happiness possible.

Jennifer's Sample Budget

To see this process in action, we'll create a budget for Jennifer, a thirty-year-old professional living in Toronto. Jennifer earns $60,000 a year. After paying $14,500 in taxes, Jennifer sets aside $10,000 toward savings and loan repayment. This leaves her with $35,500 a year to cover her expenses.

Exhibit 16 – The following budget shows how Jennifer's money is spent each month and is based on her preferences and priorities.

Step 1 – Calculate what can be spent		Step 2 & 3 – Determine how it should be spent	
Salary	$60,000	Rent	$1,350
Less taxes	$14,500	Utilities	$75
Less savings	$10,000	Groceries	$325
Annual budget	$35,500	Transportation	$250
Monthly budget	**$2,950**	Clothing	$150
		Phone and internet	$125
		Hobbies	$150
		Gifts and donations	$75
		Travel	$150
		Dining out	$200
		Miscellaneous	$100
		Total	**$2,950**

Exhibit 17 – As we can see in Jennifer's case, the 50%, 30% and 20% ratios provide a good starting point while allowing flexibility for her unique preferences.

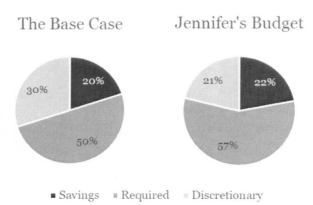

The Base Case   Jennifer's Budget

■ Savings   ■ Required   ■ Discretionary

Using Your Budget

A common misconception about budgets is that they're written in stone. Many think that if there's no money left in the entertainment bucket with five days left in the month that they're out of luck. But that's the type of limiting factor that often causes people to give up their budget or not start one in the first place. Therefore, the key to any good budget is flexibility. The plan was put in place when those categories were most important to you. If things change, change with them. Transferring money between buckets and readjusting your spending habits is only natural.

With that said, it's still important to remember your budget is there to maximize the value you receive from your money. Remaining flexible doesn't mean spending the month's budget in the first two days because that isn't going to maximize your return. It means that if you have $20 available for dinner out and you'd rather spend it on your favourite hobby, feel free. Don't feel obligated to follow the budget dollar for dollar.

Sometimes unplanned expenses can have impacts on a budget you hadn't considered. This is where the rainy day fund—mentioned in Chapter 5—comes into play. The rainy day fund is designed to protect against unexpected expenses by providing the money required in a time of need. Once you've paid for the expense, make sure to deposit savings to the fund until it's back to the desired level.

It's also important to remember that just because a dollar has been assigned to a bucket doesn't mean it has to be spent. Possibly due to unexpected savings on a purchase or a friend leaving town resulting in no dinners out, you may find yourself with extra money at the end of the month. This money can be used as you please. You may add it to your savings if you're already happy with the money you've assigned for the next month. If not, then perhaps a split between entertainment and dinners out would provide the best value for your money. Whatever bucket is decided, just remember that you can always apply current budgeted money to a future date if desired.

Final Thoughts

Creating a budget or, more broadly, any financial plan is about balance between today and tomorrow. Setting aside 50% of your money for the future at the expense of enjoying yourself today is just as bad as not saving at all. The goal is to set aside enough money to maintain your standard of living throughout your life. Celebrate the money you've earned as you spend it on things that bring you happiness, and ensure you can continue to do that in the future by setting aside an appropriate amount in savings.

A budget is meant to increase your quality of life by assigning your money to the most important expenses and ensuring you'll have enough money to last. By following the steps outlined above to develop a personal budget, you'll be better able to set money aside for the future while continuing to enjoy your day-to-day life.

Key Takeaways

- Lowering expenses is often more effective than raising your income if you want to save more.
- Set up a budget to assign your money to the most important items in your life.
- Saving money is a balance of enjoying your life today and in the future, don't sacrifice one for the other.

Chapter 7

Credit Score and Borrowing

The opportunity to borrow money today and return it some day in the future is a tempting offer. As we'll see shortly, borrowing money can be very helpful when used correctly. Too often, though, borrowing leads to poor spending habits and a debt you may not have the experience to handle. This chapter will cover the importance and steps of managing your borrowing. You'll learn how to establish credit, which is your reliability in the eyes of a lender, how your credit score—a number that represents your financial consistency—is determined and how to get out and stay out of high-interest debt. This will help you better understand the value and risks associated with the use of personal credit.

Your credit represents how capable you are of borrowing money today and consistently paying it back on time. Establishing a history of positive relationships with lenders demonstrates that you're financially responsible. This leads to several benefits. Financial institutions may offer you rewards and cash back on purchases and lower interest rates on loans. Landlords may be more likely to rent to you, and employers may be more likely to hire you.

Developing any relationship takes time for trust to build. Consider your credit score an overall value of your relationships with your current and previous lenders. As more of your borrowing encounters go well, your score will increase, and other lenders will be more likely to do business with you.

How to Build Credit

The act of building credit is a lengthy process involving several factors that demonstrate your ability to repay a loan. These factors are combined to determine a number, referred to as a credit score. Your credit score falls somewhere between 300 and 900. A higher value implies a better credit score and higher trustworthiness. If each interaction you've had with a lender was a test, your credit score would be your current grade in the class. Just as with most tests, the teacher—or credit bureau in this case—has a consistent rubric they use to assign a grade.

The aspects considered when calculating your credit score include your payment history, your current credit, your credit history, recent credit applications and the types of credit you have. All these factors contribute in some way to how you're viewed as a borrower and can therefore impact your financial situation.

Payment History

Your payment history is the most important portion of your credit score. It shows how promptly and consistently you pay back the money you've borrowed. If payments are made late to a cell phone company or credit card bill, it reflects poorly on your ability to properly borrow and pay back money. By ensuring you monitor bills coming in and pay them on time, this aspect of your credit score will gradually improve.

Current Credit

The second important factor is your current credit. This includes both how much you owe and how much you could borrow across all your lending accounts. The amount you owe is important since lenders want to know what other obligations are competing for your money. The amount you could borrow across your accounts is important because it may be more than you could reasonably pay back.

These numbers are also combined and are called your credit utilization. This is the amount you're currently borrowing relative to the total you could borrow across all your accounts. If you use all the available credit you have and then lose your job, you could have difficulty repaying your loans for a while. As a result, high utilization rates reflect poorly on your ability to repay a loan and will lower your credit score. To demonstrate, if you had a credit card with a $5,000 limit and you owed $4,500, you'd have a credit utilization of 90%. To help build a good credit score, a standard approach is to maintain a ratio that is below 30%. To achieve this, if you spend $1,200 a month on your credit card, you should aim to have a limit of at least $4,000.

Credit History

The length of your credit history is important because it's the sample size a borrower can reference when making their decision. It's harder to predict your likelihood to pay off a loan if you've only been borrowing for eight months. Therefore, start demonstrating your reliability as early as you can once you're comfortable with the responsibility. For instance, getting a student credit card is typically a good way to start the clock on your credit history.

Credit Applications

A less significant consideration is the number of recent credit applications you've made. For instance, when you apply for a new credit card or car loan, there's an entry added to your credit history. These entries are assessed in your credit score and too many can lower your score. It may suggest you're running into financial difficulty or your payment behaviour is about to change, both presenting uncertainty to lenders. While this factor often only carries temporary changes to your credit score, it's wise to limit the number of new credit cards, limit increases and loans taken out over short periods.

Forms of Credit

One final grading consideration is the different forms of credit that you have. Making payments that vary in frequency and amount demonstrates your reliability as a borrower. While this is a consideration for lenders, it's unlikely to be worth taking out additional loans to meet this category. Instead, this aspect will likely improve naturally overtime as your borrowing relationships mature.

Managing Your Credit Score

Equifax and TransUnion are the two official providers of credit scores in Canada. You can obtain your score directly from these providers or from a growing number of free online services. In addition, lenders will often look at your history to determine their own ranking of your trustworthiness. While the calculations differ across the official providers and various lenders, it's generally best to:

- only borrow what you know you can pay back
- make payments on time
- avoid maxing out your borrowing accounts
- check your credit history occasionally to ensure there are no errors

Exhibit 18 – There's no single formula used to calculate your credit score. However, the following chart provides a common breakdown of the important areas discussed above.

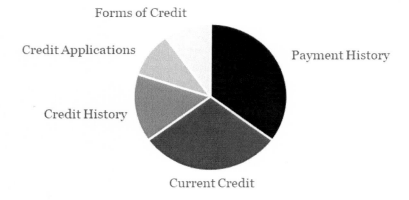

Forms of Credit

Credit Applications

Payment History

Credit History

Current Credit

Benefits of Good Credit

Now that you've seen how to manage your credit score, let's review why having good credit is valuable. The first example we'll consider is the use of various credit cards. Credit card issuers, which are often banks, earn money by receiving a fraction of the purchases made on their cards. When a credit card is used to pay for a purchase of $100, roughly $98 goes to the seller and $2 goes to the card issuer. This means credit card issuers want you to use their cards because every time you do, they make money. As a result, many credit card issuers offer rewards for using their cards. These rewards typically come in the form of cash back, travel points or deals through major companies. However, credit card issuers are only willing to offer these cards to you if you've proven yourself to be a trustworthy borrower.

The simplest of these cards to assign a dollar value to is a credit card that offers cash back on purchases. Every time a purchase is made on your cash back credit card, there are three parties being paid. The first and most obvious is the company charging you, the second, as we saw above, is the credit card issuer and the third is you. A typical cash back card offers 1% of the purchase price. This time, when that $100 sale is rung through the till, $98 goes to the seller, $1 goes to the card issuer and $1 is paid back to you. By using this credit card for day-to-day spending, those small amounts add up over time. In a year, if you charge $20,000 to a credit card offering 1% cash back, you'd earn $200.

A good credit score can also provide sizeable savings by reducing the interest rate you're charged on loans. Whether you're buying a used car or a new home, taking out a loan is a common way to obtain the money you need today. Your lender will charge you interest to be paid in addition to the original loan amount. The total interest you pay is determined by the rate of interest on the loan and how long you borrow the money for. As we've mentioned, the higher your credit score, the more trustworthy you are to lenders. As we saw in Chapter 4, the lower the risk of an investment, the lower the rate of return. Therefore, as your credit score increases, the rate of interest that you're charged typically decreases. This lower interest rate means you pay less for your loan, allowing you to put your money toward other goals.

To illustrate the impact a lower interest rate can have, let's consider two mortgages with different rates. In each case, the mortgage will be for $300,000 and will be paid back over twenty-five years. The first mortgage will be provided to an individual with a good credit score of 690, at an annual rate of 3.75%. The second mortgage is offered to an individual with an excellent credit score of 800, at an annual rate of 3.5%.

Exhibit 19 – A small difference in interest rates provided by a better credit score can lead to savings of $12,200.

Credit Score	Interest Rate	Monthly Cost	Total Interest Paid
690	3.75%	$1,542	$162,700
800	3.5%	$1,502	$150,500

If the monthly savings were invested and earned an average annual rate of 6%, they'd grow to $27,000.

As you can see from both the credit card rewards and favourable mortgage rates, there are direct cash benefits from maintaining your credit score. Following the rubric we went over earlier in this chapter will help your credit score gradually increase, providing opportunities to benefit.

Risks of Using Credit

It's important to remember that, as with any form of trust, your relationship with borrowers can be broken in a moment. As a result, ensure you can pay off a loan within the given timeframe before borrowing the money. We'll cover two common approaches to paying off debt shortly. However, if you encounter a situation where you owe money that you can't pay back, do everything in your power to address the situation. Contact your lender directly to work out a repayment plan that works for everyone or contact an alternate company to see about refinancing the debt. Regardless of how you handle the situation, remember that your credit history will impact you for better or for worse.

We mentioned in Chapter 1 that high-interest loans are very dangerous to your financial success. Paying these loans back can feel like rolling a snowball up a hill, as the interest you're charged weighs on you like gravity. Credit cards often charge interest rates as high as 20% and are one of the most common sources of high-interest debt. To avoid these interest fees, you'll need to pay off your credit card in full each month. To achieve this, make sure your credit card balance is never higher than the amount you have available in a chequing or savings account.

Most financial institutions are happy to lend you money because it means they'll earn interest from you over time. So far, we've discussed interest as a very valuable aspect of savings because it allows your money to grow. However, when you borrow, the interest you're paying is damaging to your financial situation. One way of considering interest you pay on a loan is that you're contributing to someone else's savings account. This is, of course, much less desirable than contributing to your own savings account. Because of this, it's important to avoid loans when possible, especially if they carry high interest rates or have a long payback period.

How to Get Out of Debt

It's easier said than done to avoid debt. The reality is that household borrowing in Canada continues to hit all-time highs. Student loans, mortgages and personal loans are all being used to help pay for purchases. Sometimes this is out of necessity, due to higher education costs and housing prices. And sometimes it's out of convenience, due to historically low interest rates. Whatever the source of any debt you may have, if you're looking to pay it off, there are two common approaches.

Regardless of which approach you take below, the first step for paying off debt is to see if you can refinance it. This involves finding a loan that charges a lower interest rate than what you're currently paying. If you have credit card debt charging 20% interest, it's worth seeing if you can find another loan. You may be able to get a personal loan from a bank or digital lender at a lower rate. If you borrow and pay off your credit card, you'll have an easier time paying back the new loan. It's important to ensure the rate of the new loan is lower and not a temporary offer that could increase later. Once you've refinanced any debt where it makes sense, the next step is to choose one of the following two approaches.

The first approach is to focus on your high-interest loans:

1. List your debts in order of the interest rate charged, from highest to lowest.
2. Make the minimum payment required to all loans and pay any extra you have to the highest interest loan.

3. Continue this process until you've paid off your loans.

This is helpful if your goal is to pay the least amount of interest and get out of debt the fastest.

The second approach is to focus on your small balance loans:

1. List your debts in order of the balance owed, from smallest to largest.
2. Make the minimum payment required to all loans and pay any extra you have to the smallest balance loan.
3. Continue this process until you've paid off your loans.

This is helpful if you want to see progress and simplify your debt situation by paying off individual loans faster.

Exhibit 20 – To compare these two options, let's consider Sarah who has three loans.

Loan	Amount Owed	Interest	Min Payment
Student	$28,000	6%	$200
Credit Card 1	$3,000	19%	$80
Credit Card 2	$1,000	16%	$20

We'll assume Sarah has $500 a month to pay toward debt. In both cases, she would make the minimum payment required to each loan, avoiding damage to her credit score. After paying the $300 minimum required, Sarah would have $200 remaining to apply where she sees fit.

With the first approach, the excess $200 would be paid to credit card 1 since it has the highest interest rate. Sarah would do this for a year until credit card 1 is fully paid off. From there, she'd continue paying the minimum amount for the student loan and start putting everything else toward credit card 2. Through this approach, Sarah would pay the least amount of interest and be out of debt sooner.

If Sarah chose the second approach, she'd pay extra toward credit card 2 since it has the smallest balance. Either way, the key is to pay at least the minimum required to all your loans and make extra payments as often as you can.

Common Types of Loans

From credit cards to mortgages, we've discussed quite a few types of loans thus far. To help organize them, we'll now cover the two main categories of loans. The first type is a secured loan. These require that you provide an asset, for example a house or car, to guarantee the loan. Common examples of secured loans include home mortgages and car loans. In these cases, if you can't repay your loan, the lender can recover its money by taking and selling the home or car.

The second type is an unsecured loan. These don't offer an asset for the lender to collect if you fail to repay the debt. Common examples of unsecured loans include student loans, most credit cards and bank overdrafts. Instead of securing these loans with an asset, you use your credit score to obtain them. If either loan type isn't paid back, it can have damaging effects to your credit score and future borrowing options.

When Loans Are Helpful

Some purchases require a loan since saving up enough money ahead of time often isn't reasonable. The purchase price of a home is so large, it would take quite some time to save up enough to buy one with cash. Instead, you can get a mortgage to buy and begin to live in the home today. This allows you to spread the burden of paying for the home over a more manageable period. Although a mortgage may be unavoidable, you can take steps to limit the amount of interest paid over the years.

By purchasing a home within your budget, more of your payments will go toward repaying the loan, rather than just covering interest expenses. Let's consider what would happen if you paid $1,200 a month toward two different mortgages. One is for $200,000 and another for $300,000, both charging 4% interest.

Exhibit 21 – The $200,000 mortgage is paid off in half the time, with less than a third of the interest charged.

#	Principal	Time to Repay	Interest Paid
1	$200,000	20.1 years	$89,600
2	$300,000	43.5 years	$326,400

This shows that just because you can afford to make payments on a mortgage doesn't mean the amount you're borrowing is wise. You could choose to borrow slightly less while making the same payments. By limiting the amount you borrow, you'll pay significantly less in interest and have more money to put toward earning a return of its own.

Other common uses for loans include the purchase of a car and getting a post-secondary education. In both cases, it's important to consider interest costs when deciding how much you can afford to borrow. A car with a sticker price of $10,000 ends up costing $11,400 if paid off over five years at an interest rate of 5%. Similarly, a $25,000 education financed fully through student loans would cost $33,100 if paid off over ten years at 6%.

Final Thoughts

Loans allow you to make valuable purchases well before you could otherwise. While loans are helpful, the interest costs can add up quickly. If you're not careful, the interest will begin to consume your income over time. Before taking out a loan, be sure to calculate and account for the total interest you'll pay. As we mentioned previously, paying interest is equivalent to making contributions to someone else's savings account. Avoid this when possible and instead put that money to work for yourself.

Key Takeaways

- Spend the time and effort required to build up and maintain your credit score.
- Avoid borrowing when possible, especially at high interest rates.
- Pay off debt starting with the highest interest or smallest balance, depending on your goal.

Chapter 8

Insurance and a Will

An unavoidable fact of life is that things happen unexpectedly. Occasionally, these unexpected events may result in damage to you or your belongings. Falling from a tree in the school yard and breaking an arm or forgetting a phone at a concert stadium are a few examples. While inconvenient, these events are typically only temporary setbacks on an otherwise enjoyable path through life. The need for insurance occurs when the potential damage from unexpected events goes from unpleasant to unmanageable. This typically happens at two major times: when you make larger purchases and as you develop dependents. You should consider insurance if damage or loss to a recently purchased asset would leave you financially unstable. In addition, if you have dependents— someone that relies on you for support—insurance is important to protect you from potentially losing your ability to provide for them.

Buying insurance presents a valuable tool to protect yourself from the unknown. Through relying on averages, insurance companies can take on risks that you can't handle on your own. A house burning down, a car crash or, in the worst-case scenario, death would likely leave you or your family facing financial hardship if it weren't for insurance.

Insurance companies group your situation, which presents unpredictable risks, with others in a similar situation. This forms a collection of people with a much more foreseeable and consistent level of risk. For example, while it's quite difficult to predict when any one person will pass away, the average life expectancy across a whole country is more predictable. Insurance companies don't know where or when tragedy will occur, but they can estimate what will happen on average over time. Through this process, insurance companies can take unmanageable risk off your hands for a fee.

Insurance Premiums

Insurance companies work by collecting fees, called premiums, from many customers and pooling the money together. As disaster strikes individual customers, the insurance company makes payments as outlined in the customer's insurance coverage. The premium you pay depends on the riskiness of what you're covered for. This risk depends on several factors including:

- how frequently the event happens to people in similar circumstances
- the cost if the event happens
- whether you have a deductible that you're required to pay toward the cost
- whether there's a limit to the insurance company's coverage

The following provides a common example of an insurance company collecting premiums for car insurance. A twenty-three-year-old named Jason approaches an insurance company for a quote to insure his car against the risk of a crash. The insurance company determines that the chance of a crash occurring in a month is 0.1%. They also determine the cost of the average crash to be $50,000. By multiplying the two together, the company expects its cost to insure Jason's car to be $50 a month. The insurance company may quote a $75 premium that Jason needs to pay monthly. This covers the $50 risk, operating expenses, commission for the insurance agent and the company earning a profit. The $75 is collected from numerous people all with similar risk levels. It's then set aside for the future.

After a month of collecting $75 from 1,000 customers, the insurance company has $75,000. The expected number of crashes across the 1,000 customers is one, since there was a 0.1% chance of an accident. The resulting damage of $50,000 from the crash is covered by the $75,000, and the cycle continues for each future month.

Exhibit 22 – Monthly premiums are collected and pooled together by the insurance company. When a car accident occurs, the insurance company pays the policy holder, and the remainder covers expenses and profit.

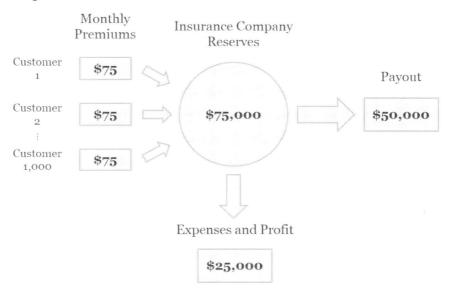

Coverage for Major Purchases

Whether you need insurance and the amount of coverage required varies from case to case. The goal is to eliminate unmanageable risk if it exists. In the case of insuring an asset such as a home or car, you'd likely want insurance to cover any expense that would leave you financially distressed. Most insurance policies have something called a deductible, which is the portion of any damage or loss that you must pay. This deductible helps minimize frivolous claims and lessens the cost to the insurance company when a payout is required. The higher your deductible, the less expensive the premium since the cost to the insurance company decreases. It's important that the deductible is an amount you can afford.

Once you've determined a reasonable deductible, you'll want to decide how much coverage you need. It's common to insure an asset for the amount it would cost to replace it with an equivalent. By insuring your assets for the cost of replacement, the only expense you'll have if something goes wrong is the deductible. If you'd like to lower your premium, you could insure the asset for less than it would cost to replace. This option is only reasonable if you're willing to take on some of the risk yourself through adjusting your lifestyle if required.

Coverage for Loss of Income

With assets now taken care of, it's time to review insurance that covers the loss of income due to disability or death. Families function through the combined efforts of every member. If the contribution from one or more member is lost, the ability for that family to function begins to falter. Once you have dependents who rely on you for their livelihood, you'll want to protect against any unmanageable risk. Disability insurance and life insurance help guarantee that your dependents are looked after financially in the event of an injury, an illness or death.

Disability Insurance

Your need for disability insurance depends on several important factors, including:

- how an injury or illness would impact the work you do
- how dependent you are on your income
- any existing coverage you have through your employer or government programs

Disability insurance can be purchased to cover you for a short-term period of three to six months or on a longer-term basis. The goal is to ensure that between all your coverage, you're able to meet your expenses while you figure out a long-term plan. If you're not sure about your needs, you can shop around between disability insurance providers to get opinions and pricing.

Life Insurance

Life insurance is a crucial step in almost all financial plans. While budgeting, saving and investing are all important, their benefits are of little help if an income provider passes away. To address this, there are two main types of life insurance available:

1. Whole life insurance, which typically provides a payout when the insured party passes away or at a predefined maturity age

2. Term life insurance, which provides a payout only if the insured party passes away during a defined period, usually ranging from ten to thirty years

Whole Life Insurance

With whole life insurance, premiums are more expensive because it's a combination of pure insurance coverage and a savings product. Over time, the policy builds cash value because the amount you're paying in premiums is partially going toward investments. While this may sound attractive, the fees charged on the investments are often higher than you can find elsewhere.

Term Life Insurance

With term life insurance, you purchase insurance coverage only, and as a result, it's less expensive. A common approach is to select term life insurance and to put the savings from the lower premium into investments yourself. This way you have life insurance and maintain control over how your savings are invested. A second benefit to term life insurance is that as your coverage needs change, which is common as your savings grow and dependents shift, you can adjust the amount of insurance you're purchasing.

Term life insurance works similarly to the previously discussed car insurance example. Based on your age, gender, health conditions and other factors, the insurance company determines the cost to provide coverage. This includes the likelihood that you could pass away over the length of the ten to thirty-year term. Combining this likelihood and the coverage of your insurance, which is the amount the company pays if you should pass away, provides the expected cost to the insurance provider. Adding the expected cost to the expenses we outlined previously determines the premiums required to take on the risk.

Premiums are then charged over the period of the term at a constant rate. If a payment is required due to your passing, it's provided to the beneficiary named in the insurance plan. If you survive through the term of the insurance coverage—as is often expected to be the case—then no money is paid by the insurance company. While the company may not pay out in most cases, they've done their job of removing an unmanageable risk off your hands.

Calculating the Coverage Needed

The most important number to consider when purchasing life insurance is the amount of coverage you need. This number determines how much you'll pay in premiums and is how much your family will receive in the event of your passing. It's important that you take the time to calculate what you need. Too much coverage leads to unnecessarily high premiums, and too little coverage could lower your family's standard of living. To demonstrate how to calculate the amount of insurance coverage needed and to show how this coverage may change overtime, we'll consider an example involving a family of four.

Life Insurance for a Family of Four

Today the family in question lives comfortably on a combined income of $80,000 after tax. They're setting aside savings, making payments toward their mortgage and have two cars in the driveway that are nearly paid off. If either parent was to pass without life insurance in place, the damage to the remaining family's well-being would be substantial.

There are two common ways the family can determine how much coverage they need. We'll refer to these options as the income formula and the expense formula.

Option One: Income Formula

The first option is to calculate how much income the family needs going forward if either parent was to pass away. To do this, the following steps are required:

1. Determine what portion of expenses today will no longer be required if a parent passed. For example, retirement savings or transportation costs for that parent would no longer be required. In our case, we'll assume this is $15,000.

2. Subtract this amount from the total income earned today to determine what you would need going forward. In this case, they'd need $80,000 minus $15,000 for a total of $65,000.

3. Subtract the income of the surviving spouse to determine what needs to be provided by insurance. Here, we'll assume each parent earns $40,000, so the amount needed from insurance is $25,000.

4. Assume that the income is needed until the parent would otherwise have retired. We'll assume this is a period of twenty-five years.

5. Multiply the income required by the number of years to determine the total coverage. In this case, the $25,000 is multiplied by twenty-five years for a total of $625,000.

With $625,000 in coverage, the family would have access to $25,000 a year for the next twenty-five years. There may be minor adjustments to this amount for inflation or the growth rate that could be earned on the money, but it provides a good approximation.

Option Two: Expense Formula

The second option is to account for major future expenses. To do this, the following steps are required:

1. Identify a list of future expenses that need to be paid for from the insurance coverage. In the case of the family of four, this may include:
   - Post-secondary school for both children
   - The remainder of the mortgage
   - Funeral and burial
   - Retirement savings for the surviving spouse

2. Determine the cost of each item on the list. For our purposes, we'll make the following assumptions:
   - Education - $80,000
   - Mortgage - $225,000
   - Funeral - $10,000
   - Retirement - $250,000

3. Add up the list to find the total coverage required. With the expense base approach, the family would require $565,000.

With an initial payment of $565,000 to take care of major expenses, the parents may decide they could each manage with their current income of $40,000.

Coverage Needs Over Time

The family may find that the amount of coverage they calculate will be suitable up until the parents are forty-five. At that point, they could reassess their financial situation to determine the amount required for the next insurance term. In this instance, it's clear to see why it's attractive to break your insurance policies into multiple periods. As the years go by with both parents contributing to savings, the amount of insurance coverage required shrinks. Once the children are all finished with university, for instance, that's coverage that is no longer required. By re-evaluating your financial needs regularly and purchasing the right coverage to protect against the worst-case scenario, you can live with peace of mind.

Life Insurance Policy Structures

One important thing to remember when purchasing life insurance is the way it's structured. For instance, if the father in our case needed extra income to support the family going forward, then the insurance policy would be taken out by the mother. The father would be named as the beneficiary, which is the person that receives the money. That way, in the event of the mother's passing, the required amount of insurance would be provided to the father. Another instance that's important to consider is the event both parents pass away together. You'll want to ensure that your policies are set up so there's no risk that any surviving party will go without the required financial support.

Creating a Will

In addition to getting insurance, it's often wise to create a will as your net worth increases, you marry or have dependents. If you pass away without a will in Canada, the laws of your province or territory will determine how your estate is handled. To have more control over your estate, including how your money is divided, you can set up a will. Nowadays, this can be done online or in person with assistance from a professional. Over time, it's important to revisit your will to keep it up to date with your situation and intentions.

Final Thoughts

Protecting yourself against unmanageable risk is crucial to a successful financial plan. This can be done by setting up a will and purchasing the right insurance. You can determine what's suitable for your needs by speaking with several insurance providers. With so many risks to consider—death, injury, illness, theft and damages— you'll want to know what's needed and what's optional. Shopping around for insurance is beneficial since different companies place emphasis on different factors. This often results in different pricing for the same coverage. If you're sure the coverage is equal in both cases, selecting the lower premium will help save money.

Some insurance providers offer additional services, like double coverage in the event of an accidental death, at little additional cost. Remember that the point of insurance is to cover your damages or loss of income—no more, no less. By purchasing the required coverage at the best possible rate, you'll be prepared for the unknown while paying the lowest price possible.

Key Takeaways

- Insurance and a will are crucial to your financial plan to protect against unmanageable risks.
- Disability insurance and life insurance are important if you have dependents.
- Shop around for the best rate and avoid add-ons that you don't need.

Chapter 9

The Registered Retirement
Savings Plan (RRSP)

One of the most important goals people have is being financially stable in retirement. To achieve this, you could deposit your savings in a traditional bank account, like you would if saving for a new TV. Or you could take advantage of specialized savings accounts designed for people saving for retirement. With these specialized accounts, your money will grow faster and larger.

An account that's specifically designed to help you save for retirement is the Registered Retirement Savings Plan (RRSP). The Canadian Government recognizes the importance of retirement savings for a country's well-being. Therefore, they offer a series of incentives to encourage you to plan and save for the future. The RRSP is a tremendous option for retirement savings because you can postpone paying taxes until you withdraw.

In addition to the tax benefits, there are several features that make the RRSP versatile for other savings goals. The Home Buyers' Plan (HBP) and Lifelong Learning Plan (LLP) allow you to use your savings temporarily for other purposes. We'll cover these features in greater detail shortly, but first, let's discuss the tax benefits of the RRSP.

Postponing Taxes

The benefit of postponing taxes through an RRSP is best demonstrated by breaking it up into its two components:

1. You don't pay income tax on money deposited to an RRSP until it's withdrawn, most often in retirement.

2. Your money grows tax free while in the account.

Most people earn a higher income while saving for retirement than they do in retirement. As a result, the taxes you'd pay on income today may be higher than the tax you'll pay if you wait until retirement. The tax benefit of postponing your income is an instant return on your savings. In addition, because your savings grow tax free while in the account, your balance will increase faster than with a traditional savings account.

Exhibit 23 – The RRSP's main benefit comes from postponing income taxes and taxes on growth until the money is withdrawn. The below comparison demonstrates how it differs from a traditional savings account.

Postponing Income Tax

Deposits made to your RRSP account can be used to reduce your income. Lowering your income then reduces the amount of taxes you owe to the government. This often results in a tax refund because you've likely payed taxes throughout the year on your full income. The value of the refund depends on how much you deposit to the RRSP and your income tax rate. The higher the income tax rate, the higher the benefit of the RRSP.

Take, for instance, Emma, who deposits $2,000 to her RRSP. Since the $2,000 can be deducted from her income, she'd receive a refund for taxes already paid. If the tax rate charged on the $2,000 was 35%, then she'd receive a refund of $700. This results in a deposit of $2,000 into the RRSP that has technically only cost Emma $1,300. If she hadn't deposited the $2,000 into her RRSP, she'd have paid taxes on it and would only have $1,300 left.

The government helps establish your RRSP now, knowing the money will be taxed when withdrawn. As we mentioned before, the tax rate charged when the money is withdrawn may be lower than what would have been paid today. In Emma's case, she now has $2,000 in her account that cost her $1,300. If in retirement she's charged 25% in taxes on the withdrawal, she'd be left with $1,500. Therefore, the equivalent of $1,300 without an RRSP has turned into $1,500 with the account. This potential difference in tax rates between today and retirement allows you to save more money by using an RRSP.

Tax-Free Growth

The second way you postpone tax is because growth in an RRSP account isn't taxed until the money is withdrawn. Therefore, instead of your savings being taxed yearly, resulting in slower growth, the money grows tax free until it's needed in retirement.

To demonstrate just how beneficial tax-free growth is, let's revisit Emma's case and consider growth on her deposit. Remembering back to the $2,000 contribution, what resulted was a cost of $1,300 to Emma and $700 that came from the government in the way of a tax refund. This means that of the $2,000 currently in the account, $700—or 35%—can be considered from the government.

This idea of distinguishing between the cost of the contribution and the government's refund is not a common practice. I'm using these labels to illustrate how money flows through an RRSP to properly demonstrate the total value of the account. The full balance of an RRSP is considered the account holder's money. They're required to pay taxes only when a withdrawal is made. I'm using the term "the government's portion" purely to help understand why RRSPs are so valuable.

In our case above, 65% of the account came from Emma and 35% came from the government. The RRSP account begins with an initial value of $2,000. If the savings grew at 7% a year for thirty years, the balance would reach $15,225. Paying 25% in taxes would result in a balance of $11,418.

Now let's consider if the $1,300, which was Emma's share of the deposit, grew tax free for thirty years at 7%. The savings would reach $9,896. You'll notice that you earn more with an RRSP even though you're paying taxes on your growth when you withdraw. This is because you also get to use the government's portion of the account.

We can consider the government's contribution to be the $700 tax refund. This $700 grows in the account for thirty years at 7%. The government's portion reaches a value of $5,329 by the time retirement arrives. As we saw previously, the tax charged on the withdrawal from the RRSP is only $3,806. This is the 25% tax charged on the total withdrawal of $15,225.

Therefore, when you're taxed in retirement, provided the tax rate being charged is less than your tax rate when you claimed your contribution, the government isn't even taking back the taxes they were originally entitled to. In other words, you keep your original cost of $1,300 plus all the gains made on that deposit. As if that wasn't enough, the government allows you to keep a portion of their share of the growth.

Exhibit 24 – You keep your net contribution, all the growth on it and even some of the growth from the government's refund. This assumes the tax rate you pay in retirement is lower than your rate when depositing.

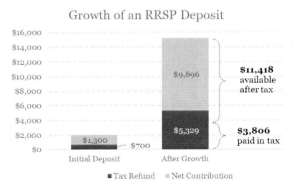

Growth of an RRSP Deposit

Your Income Tax Rates

The most important considerations with an RRSP are the tax rates while you're depositing the money and when it's withdrawn. All throughout the previous example, we assumed the rate charged today is higher than the rate in retirement. If this is the case, the benefits of postponing tax through an RRSP are clear. However, if you expect to be charged a higher tax rate in retirement than you are today, then more analysis is required. There's still the benefit of tax-free growth in the account. But as the tax rate you expect in retirement increases compared to your current rate, the value of the account diminishes.

We've now covered the most common and obvious use of the RRSP: to help people save for their retirement. The next two features allow you to use the account for other goals.

The Home Buyers' Plan (HBP)

The HBP allows you to withdraw from your RRSP to help with the purchase of your first home. To be eligible, you can't have owned a home within the last five years or have an outstanding balance from a previous HBP. As we discussed in Emma's case above, let's consider the government's tax credit to be their portion of the RRSP. The HBP allows you to borrow the government's money with no interest expense to buy your home. By depositing money into an RRSP and receiving the tax refund and then withdrawing the money through the HBP, you'll have more available for your down payment.

To demonstrate, let's consider Susan, who plans to purchase a home in three years with savings she'll start setting aside today. For simplicity, we'll assume no growth is earned on the savings and focus on the HBP alone. Susan's net income is $65,000 a year, which results in a marginal tax rate of 40%. The marginal tax rate is the rate of tax she paid on the last dollar she earned, which we'll learn more about in Chapter 17. Of the $65,000 after-tax income, she needs $60,000 for other savings and living expenses each year. Without an RRSP, Susan places $5,000 a year into a savings account for three years, reaching a balance of $15,000.

However, if Susan used her RRSP, she could collect more money for her down payment. For every $1,000 Susan contributes to her RRSP, she'll receive a tax refund of $400, since she's already paid

40% in taxes. Therefore, if Susan contributes $8,333 to her RRSP, she'll receive a tax refund of $3,333. This leaves Susan with $8,333 in her RRSP and still provides $60,000 for her other needs for the year. If she follows these same steps for the three-year period, she would collect $25,000 in her RRSP. Susan can then withdraw the $25,000 from the RRSP to make the purchase of her new home. The additional $10,000 reduces costs associated with a home purchase, such as mortgage insurance and interest.

Exhibit 25 – By depositing $5,000 into a traditional account or $8,333 to an RRSP, Susan has $60,000 available for her other needs. However, with an RRSP, Susan collects $25,000 over three years for her home purchase instead of $15,000.

	No RRSP	**With RRSP**
After-tax income	$65,000	$65,000
Less deposit	**$5,000**	**$8,333**
Plus tax rebate	N/A	$3,333
Available to spend	$60,000	$60,000

HBP Guidelines

In 2019, the maximum withdrawal was increased from $25,000 to $35,000. A contribution must be made to the RRSP ninety days before it's used for the HBP to still be tax deductible. You receive a two-year grace period after the money is withdrawn before you must start repaying the HBP. After the two years are over, the money must be repaid over the next fifteen years. Each year, you must deposit the outstanding balance divided by the number of years remaining to repay it. For instance, two years after Susan's $25,000 withdrawal, she must deposit at least $1,667 per year back into her RRSP. Susan could choose to pay it back at a faster rate if desired. Each year, the required deposit is recalculated as the outstanding balance divided by the number of years remaining to pay it back.

If you don't deposit the required minimum back into your RRSP, there are costs. The difference between the minimum and the amount contributed must be counted as taxable income in that year. If Susan contributes $667 instead of the full $1,667 her first year, she'd need to add $1,000 to her income and pay the required taxes. In addition to paying tax on the $1,000, Susan can't recontribute this money in the future. Since contribution room to an RRSP is valuable, it's wise to try and repay at least the minimum amount each year. Any contribution made to repay the HBP is no longer tax deductible since the original contribution that was withdrawn already received that benefit.

The Lifelong Learning Plan (LLP)

The LLP allows you to withdraw from an RRSP to pursue additional schooling. Like the HBP, the major benefit is that you'll have more money available if you use your RRSP than if you don't. It's possible to save on loans by withdrawing temporarily from an RRSP instead. With the LLP, the maximum annual withdrawal is $10,000, with a cumulative maximum of $20,000. There's typically a grace period of five years from the year of the first withdrawal where repayments aren't required. After the five-year grace period, you'd have an additional ten years to repay the LLP following similar rules as the HBP.

RRSP Guidelines

We've now covered in depth the benefits of contributing to an RRSP. Next, let's discuss some of the rules and guidelines for depositing. Anyone that has earned contribution room can deposit to an RRSP up until the year of their seventy-first birthday. Each year, you earn 18% of your previous year's reported income in contribution room. This means with an income of $50,000, you'd earn $9,000 in contribution room. The amount of contribution room is capped by an annual limit that's determined each year. For reference, in 2018, the maximum contribution room that could be earned was $26,230. This meant anyone with income below $145,722 earned 18% of their income in contribution room. Anyone earning more than $145,722 was capped out by the $26,230 maximum. Any contribution room that is earned and not used each year can be carried forward for future use.

Since unused contribution room is carried forward to future years, you'll often have a buildup of available room. Whether from summer jobs or other income, you can use this room to start contributing to your RRSP. You can find out what your available contribution room is from the Canada Revenue Agency, which we'll cover in Chapter 19.

As we've mentioned, deposits to your RRSP allow you to lower your income, reducing the taxes you owe. However, you can choose when to lower your income. You can choose to lower your income the same year you make a deposit, or you can wait to lower your income in a future year. It's rare to wait to lower your income for a future year, but it can help you gain additional tax savings when the right circumstances strike. For instance, if you only work six months out of the year due to school or a sabbatical, your income will be lower for the year. If you have money and contribution room available, you can still deposit to your RRSP and wait to lower your income until a future year. By waiting until the next year when your income and tax rate are likely to be higher, you'll receive a greater tax benefit.

RRSP Investment Options

We've now seen how your savings benefit from being in an RRSP and how to go about depositing your money. Next, we'll review the investment options available to help your money grow. Stocks, guaranteed investment certificates (GICs), bonds, exchange-traded funds (ETFs) and mutual funds—all of which will be covered shortly—are common investments used in an RRSP.

Depending on the chosen investment option, your required workload and knowledge level will differ. Individual stocks and bonds can be combined in a range of ways to meet most investment needs. However, a higher level of attention and knowledge is often required if you buy them individually. If you'd prefer a simpler approach, then ETFs or mutual funds provide an already bundled option. These funds are managed by experienced professionals and combine stocks and bonds for you. Whether you take a hands-on approach or rely on professionals, the important part is that your investments are growing tax free while in the RRSP.

Registered Retirement Income Fund (RRIF)

After years of saving in an RRSP, the goal is to eventually use the money for your expenses in retirement. To do this, you'll need to withdraw from the account. Money in an RRSP can be withdrawn or transferred into an RRIF—read as rif—at any point in time. However, it's most commonly done once you reach retirement. Any withdrawal—aside from special circumstances, such as the HBP and LLP discussed above—made from an RRSP or RRIF is considered taxable income. This means you'll need to report the withdrawal and pay taxes in the year of the withdrawal. These withdrawals are taxable because you received a tax refund when the initial deposit was made to the RRSP. You postponed paying income taxes when you earned the money and are now required to pay them on the withdrawal.

Often your financial institution will withhold part of the withdrawal and send the money directly to the Canada Revenue Agency. This is like how income tax is withheld and paid on your behalf by your employer. However, the amount withheld by your financial institution often isn't the total amount you'll owe. Therefore, it's important to consider how much tax you'll eventually owe on any withdrawal from an RRSP or RRIF.

Your RRSP must be closed by December 31 of the year you turn seventy-one. Most often, the money in an RRSP is transferred into a RRIF and gradually withdrawn throughout retirement. However, the money can also be used to purchase an annuity, or it can be withdrawn, likely resulting in significant taxes. Once the RRSP is closed and the money is transferred to a RRIF, no more deposits can be made.

Each year, there's a minimum withdrawal required from the RRIF. The amount required is calculated based on the value of the account at the start of the year and your age. You can withdraw more than the minimum, but as we mentioned above, these withdrawals are taxable income. Therefore, the more you withdraw in any given year, the higher the tax obligation. Since you'll likely have income from other sources, it's worth spending some time each year to determine the most tax efficient approach.

Final Thoughts

Saving for your retirement can feel like a daunting task. With compound growth from investments and the tax advantages of an RRSP, it's much more manageable. If your current income tax rate is higher than you expect it will be in retirement, then an RRSP is a very useful tool. However, if you expect your income to increase in the years ahead, there's another account that may be better suited for you. Our next chapter will cover the Tax-Free Savings Account (TFSA). This account provides another great option to help you save for retirement. We'll provide a list of similarities and differences between the RRSP and TFSA to help you decide which is right for you.

Key Takeaways

- Postpone paying higher income taxes today by depositing money to an RRSP.
- Invest in any of a broad range of options to grow your money tax free while in the account.
- Manage your withdrawals from an RRSP or RRIF to avoid paying excess taxes.

Chapter 10

The Tax-Free Savings Account (TFSA)

Retirement savings are a common and often significant portion of money set aside for the future. However, there are plenty of other reasons you may want to save money. A downside to putting savings in a traditional bank account is that growth earned over time is taxable. This tax can have a significant impact on the speed at which your savings grow. As a result, we'll discuss another type of account that offers tax advantages and more flexibility than the RRSP.

A Tax-Free Savings Account (TFSA) is a fantastic option when setting aside money for any goal. It can be used for short-term savings toward a car or vacation, medium-term savings for a house or long-term savings to supplement or replace an RRSP in preparing for retirement. It has significantly fewer rules than an RRSP, providing flexibility to meet your needs. The benefit of a TFSA is that any growth on the money held in the account is tax free. This allows for much faster growth of your savings relative to holding them in a traditional savings account.

Traditional savings accounts can also be referred to as non-registered accounts. TFSAs, RRSPs and other accounts with tax advantages are registered with the Canadian Government. A traditional savings account without tax benefits isn't registered and is therefore called a non-registered account.

Exhibit 26 – This graphic demonstrates that a TFSA completely removes tax on growth. Since growth is tax free, your savings compound at a faster rate, resulting in more money for your goals.

Traditional Savings Account	VS.	TFSA

Traditional Savings Account:
Income Earned ⇩ Taxed on Income ⇩ Savings Invested ⇩ Savings Growth ⇩ **Taxed on Growth** ⇩ Growth Reinvested ⇩ Money Withdrawn

TFSA:
Income Earned ⇩ Taxed on Income ⇩ Savings Invested ⇩ Savings Growth ⇩ Growth Reinvested ⇩ Money Withdrawn

The TFSA was introduced in 2009 and is offered to Canadians eighteen years of age or older. The annual contribution limit in 2009 was $5,000, and it has increased over time. This increase is to account for inflation, which we discussed in Chapter 5. As of 2021, the annual contribution limit is $6,000. You begin earning contribution room when you turn eighteen, and any unused room carries forward indefinitely. Therefore, anyone born in 1991 or earlier who hasn't deposited to a TFSA has $75,500 in contribution room as of January 1, 2021.

TFSA Benefits

A TFSA is more flexible than an RRSP. For one, withdrawals from a TFSA aren't taxed. In addition, the amount you withdraw is added back to your contribution room the following calendar year. For instance, if you have $30,000 in a TFSA and withdraw $4,500, you can do so with no penalties or taxes. The following calendar year, you receive the $4,500 back as available contribution room, in addition to the new yearly limit.

The remarkable benefit of the TFSA is that growth on investments in the account are free of tax. This benefit was mentioned in the previous exhibit and the magnitude of the benefit is described through the following two examples. Growth on your investments is normally taxed if held in a traditional savings account. The amount of taxes you're required to pay depends on the type of growth and your income, which we'll cover in Chapter 17. The benefit of the TFSA is that you don't need to worry about those factors since there's no tax.

To demonstrate just how valuable this is, let's consider $20,000 in a traditional bank account earning 2% interest. The first year, the account earns $400 in interest, which is taxed just like your regular income. In any given year, the taxes may seem small. However, as we saw in Chapter 2, a small change to your compound growth rate has a significant impact on the end value of your savings. This is especially true over long periods of time.

Let's continue the process of earning interest and paying taxes— assuming a tax rate of 30%—on that interest for thirty years. With annual tax on the interest, the $20,000 grows to a value of $30,350. Now, if the $20,000 were placed in a TFSA, where it can grow tax free, the account would grow to $36,230.

Exhibit 27 – We'll use the flow from Exhibit 26 and focus on how much is deposited and how much is withdrawn in each case.

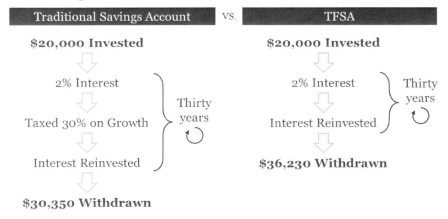

To compare the difference in growth between the two accounts, we'll subtract the initial $20,000 from the ending balances. With the traditional account, a total of $10,350 is earned, and with a TFSA, $16,230 is earned. In the simplest of comparisons, assuming a low rate of return and a reasonable tax bracket, the TFSA results in 50% more growth. From this, it's clear the TFSA offers significant value. However, if you're not yet convinced, the next example will assume a higher return through investing in the stock market.

For simplicity, the following example includes the purchase of the same bundle of stocks in both a traditional account and in a TFSA. Once again, we'll begin with a $20,000 deposit. This time, we'll deposit in a brokerage account—a standard account used for investing in stocks, bonds and exchange-traded funds—to purchase the stocks.

After thirty years, at an average annual growth rate of 7%, the initial deposit of $20,000 grows to $152,250. The growth of $132,250 is considered a capital gain. With the current tax system in Canada, half of the gain is added to your yearly income and taxed as usual. Assuming a tax rate of 30%, a total of $19,840 would be owed in taxes. If this same investment were made in a TFSA, there would be no taxes charged. Therefore, you'd have an additional $19,840 toward your goal.

Over-Contributing

It's important to keep track of your contribution limit for the TFSA to avoid depositing more than you're allowed. While it would be nice to deposit all your savings in a TFSA, the taxes we pay provide a great deal of good for our country. There's a constant balance being struck with accounts like the RRSP and TFSA between incenting people to save and collecting a regular stream of taxes. To manage this balance, there's a penalty if you over-contribute to your account, whether by accident or not. The current penalty for over-contributing is 1% of the overage per calendar month. If your contribution limit is $20,000 and you contribute $21,000, then you'd owe $10 a month until the error is corrected.

TFSA vs. RRSP

We've now covered two savings accounts that can assist with long-term savings for retirement. Both the RRSP and TFSA are very helpful in maximizing your personal wealth. The question that may now arise is which account is better to use. The exact answer to this question requires information on your personal circumstances, some speculation about the future and a bit of calculation. While an exact answer isn't possible on a general basis, there are several factors that can give you a good sense of which account is right for you.

Exhibit 28 – The following table summarizes the main similarities and differences between a TFSA and an RRSP. Withdrawals in the table don't include the HBP or LLP, which follow different rules that were discussed previously.

	Question	TFSA	RRSP
Similarities	Can I carry forward contribution room?	Yes	Yes
	Am I taxed on growth within the account?	No	No
	What investments can I use in the account?	Options in this book and more	Options in this book and more
Differences	Are my deposits tax deductible?	No	Yes
	Am I taxed on withdrawals?	No	Yes
	How much contribution room do I earn each year?	$6,000 as of 2019	18% of income up to annual max
	Are withdrawals added back to my contribution room?	Yes, the following calendar year	No
	Am I required to transfer money from the account?	No	Yes, year of 71st birthday
	When can I start depositing money?	18 or 19, age of majority	Once room is earned
	Are there additional features to the account?	No	Yes, HBP and LLP

Differences: When You Pay Income Tax

We'll begin by outlining the main difference between the TFSA and the RRSP. A TFSA requires you to pay taxes on your income before you can deposit your money. An RRSP allows you to deposit money before you've paid income tax, but it requires you pay taxes when you withdraw.

Exhibit 29 – We can see that the key difference is whether you're taxed before the deposit is made or after the money is withdrawn.

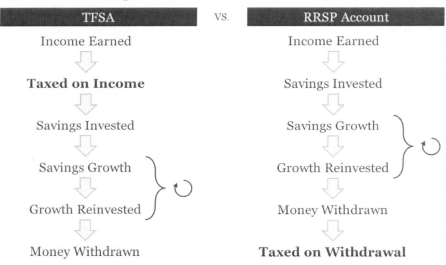

If you expect a lower tax rate in retirement than you'd pay today, then the advantage goes to the RRSP. For instance, you may receive a tax rebate for 30% of your deposit to an RRSP and only pay 20% tax when you withdraw. In this case, you'd have more than 10% additional money for retirement by using an RRSP.

Exhibit 30 – The below flow shows the above case if you set aside $7,000 of income and earn 6% growth for twenty years.

With the RRSP and a lower tax rate in retirement, you'd have $18,000 rather than $15,700 with the TFSA. However, since tax rates have varied throughout history, there's no guarantee what you'll pay in retirement. With that in mind, favouring a TFSA will provide a more certain amount for retirement spending. You won't be dependent on future tax rates because you'll have paid everything up front.

Differences: Accessibility of Your Money

The second consideration is how accessible your money is in each account. As we've seen, a TFSA allows you to withdraw money at any time with no penalties or taxes. You can even redeposit immediately after if you have the contribution room available. If not, you'll be able to redeposit in any future calendar year. An RRSP, on the other hand, has a much more restrictive set of withdrawal rules. Whether restrictions to withdrawals are a good or bad thing is dependent on you. If you can resist the temptation to spend money in a TFSA until you've reached your goal, then the flexibility is great. However, if you'd prefer to know your money is harder to spend, then the RRSP has the advantage.

Differences: Other Considerations

Several other considerations include taking advantage of the HBP or LLP or figuring out how your income in retirement could impact government pension payments. Certain pension income is provided to lower-income retirees. If you have high income in retirement due to withdrawals from an RRSP or RRIF, you may receive less from the government.

The general theme is that a TFSA provides the greatest flexibility and certainty of what you'll have in retirement. Meanwhile, the RRSP offers several unique features that can increase the amount you'll have in certain cases. One approach is to start with a TFSA. Over time, if your circumstances call for it—if you find you're paying a high tax rate or could use the HBP or LLP—you can withdraw money from your TFSA and transfer it to an RRSP.

Final Thoughts

Regardless of which account you start with, if you reach your contribution limit, the next step is to switch your attention to the other account. If you find yourself in this situation, you've done a tremendous job setting yourself up for a great retirement. Steady contributions to a TFSA and/or an RRSP will help you reach your savings goals. It will also ensure the hard work you're putting in to earn your income today will pay off well into the future. Adding these accounts to your financial plan is like adding a pair of twigs and a black top hat to a snowman.

Key Takeaways

- Reduce your taxes and have more money for any goal using your TFSA.
- Start with a TFSA for retirement savings until you've determined if an RRSP is right for your needs.
- Monitor your contribution limit to avoid paying unnecessary fees.

Chapter 11

Employer Retirement Plan

There are many ways employers compete to attract talented employees to work with them. The most obvious method is paying them through hourly wages or annual salaries. In addition, health and dental insurance, wellness plans, paid vacation, parental leave and retirement plans can help attract and retain talent. Many employers offer retirement plans to help their employees save for the future. We'll briefly discuss the different ways these plans can be designed before going in depth on some of the most common options.

Plan Designs

Employers can offer retirement plans that use either an RRSP or TFSA as the foundation. They can also use a Registered Pension Plan (RPP), which is a specific account type available to employers. Aside from the account type used, there are two distinct types of pension plans: defined benefit and defined contribution.

Defined benefit plans specify how much you'll receive in the future. This amount is typically based on the number of years you work at the company and your salary leading up to retirement.

Defined contribution plans don't specify future payments. Instead, they depend on the contributions made and performance of the investments. Defined contribution plans are more common these days. One benefit for the employer is that they reduce risk by removing the need to guarantee future payments. Unfortunately for the employee, they add uncertainty to retirement earnings and make it more important than ever to plan.

Several other considerations for employer retirement plans include:

- whether you're required or able to contribute yourself
- whether there's a waiting period before you can join
- what investments are available
- whether there's a vesting period before you have full claim to the money

With the nuances of employer plans covered, let's discuss the most common plans. You may currently have access to one of these plans or could see them in the future.

Common Plans

The first is a defined contribution pension plan, where the employer matches 100% of your contributions up to a maximum percentage of your salary. The maximum matching might start out at 2% and grow to 5% based on your tenure with the company. Let's see how this plan would work for you if your yearly income was $60,000.

In the first year of signing up, you'd contribute the maximum matching of 2%. You'd set aside $1,200, and your employer would match it with an additional $1,200. Assuming you're paid every two weeks, you'd set aside just $46 a paycheque. At the end of the year, you'd have $2,400 in savings. This 100% matching is the equivalent of a 100% return on your investment the moment you set the money aside. Even at 7% annual returns, it would take just over ten years to reach 100%. This demonstrates why employer plans can be so valuable to your retirement savings.

Another plan is a group RRSP where your employer matches 50% of your contributions to a set maximum. In this case, the employer may match your contributions up to 6% of your salary. Assuming the same salary and pay cycle as above, you'd set aside $138 a paycheque. By year end, you'd have contributed $3,600 to your account. Your employer's 50% matching would add $1,800, resulting in $5,400 total. If you continue for twenty-five years and your investments grew at an average annual rate of 6%, you'd have $296,300.

Speak to Your Employer

The first step is to find out if your employer provides a group retirement or pension plan. Not all employers offer them since, as we saw before, it's one of many factors that they consider. There's an alphabet soup of different names for employer retirement plans. Whether it's an RPP, Group RRSP or TFSA, Employee Share Plan (ESP), Deferred Profit Sharing Plan (DPSP) or another option, your HR team should know what's available.

The next step is to find out whether your employer makes contributions to the account. If the employer doesn't make contributions, there's less value in signing up. However, if they make contributions, there's a great deal of value in signing up. Your employer may only deposit if you make contributions as well, or they may contribute without you needing to do anything. Either way, employer contributions are part of your total compensation package, and it's important to take advantage. The final step is to make sure you're contributing as much as you need to max out any matching from your employer.

Choosing Your Investment Fund

Once you've signed up and determined the amount you'll contribute, it's time to decide how you'll invest. As we discussed in Chapter 4, you'll want to consider the length of time you have until retirement. By taking on an appropriate amount of risk, you can help your savings grow and reach what you'll need for retirement.

A common investment option in employer plans is a target date fund. These funds automatically rebalance your investments over time to reduce the level of risk as you approach retirement. We saw this process in Chapter 4 when Katelyn gradually switched from 10% low risk to 50% as she approached retirement.

Depending on your plan, you may also have access to the usual investment options discussed throughout this book. Important things to consider include:

- Your level of involvement
  - Funds and professional advisors offer the option to be more hands-off.

- The fees you're paying
  - Funds and professional advisors charge a fee that can significantly impact your growth if it's too high.
- The risk you're taking
  - Saving for retirement usually offers a long period to invest, providing the opportunity to take on more risk.

Additional Benefits

One major benefit of employer plans is that the money is taken off your paycheque at the source. This automates the process and makes saving less painful. In addition, it's easier to leave this money out of sight and out of mind. As we mentioned before, it's important not to try to time the market or fret over the ups and downs, and these plans help with that. Employer matching, the automated process and a less accessible account make these plans excellent for retirement savings.

If you leave your employer before retirement, which is becoming more common, you can transfer your plan in several different ways. Depending on your circumstances and the value of the plan, you may be able to:

- transfer it to a plan with a new employer
- transfer to a Locked-In Retirement Account (LIRA) or other registered account
- take a cash disbursement

Final Thoughts

As we mentioned in Chapter 1, start where you're comfortable and increase your contributions gradually. The sooner you contribute the maximum your employer will match, the better. 50% or 100% returns are the equivalent of saving you six or ten years of growth instantly. It's the easiest way to catch up if you're starting to save later than you'd like and a great way to get ahead if you're early in your career.

Key Takeaways

- Find out from your employer if they offer retirement plans and whether they make contributions.

- Deposit enough to the plan to get the full matching from your employer.
- Payroll deductions let you get to your money first, automate the process and keep your money out of sight.

Chapter 12

The Stock Market

As we began to cover in Chapter 3, there are lots of ways you can earn a higher rate of return on your savings. We mentioned that most options fall into the two categories of buying ownership or lending your money. One option is to own part of a company by purchasing shares. The company takes your savings, invests them in its business and pays you back in the future. If you're dealing with shares of multiple companies, they're called stocks. The stock market provides a marketplace where you can go to buy and sell stocks.

People typically have one of two reactions when they hear the words "stock market." Some think it's a way to make quick money and are keen to dive right in. Others think it's the fastest way to lose your savings and avoid it at all costs. It requires the combination of these views to best benefit from investing in stocks. After all, the stock market offers an excellent way to potentially grow your money while managing your risk. In Chapter 3, we mentioned you can minimize your risk by diversifying and investing for a long period of time.

How Shares Work

To understand how a share works, we'll consider a boy looking to set up a snow cone stand in his neighbourhood. He needs money to start his business—to buy a stand, cups and syrup. He's done his research and knows that it should cost $40 to buy everything he needs. One small issue, however, is that he doesn't have the money needed to get started. As a result, he approaches his brother and sister to ask for $20 from each of them. In exchange for their money, the boy offers them each 25% ownership in his snow cone business.

Both siblings agree and pay their brother $20 to help him set up shop. The 25% ownership that each sibling now has is considered their share of the company. Their share represents the claim to a portion of any profits the snow cone stand earns in the future. While this is a simplified example, shares in the stock market follow a very similar format. They provide you a claim to a portion of the company's future profits and assets, which may include cash, buildings, patents and more.

There's one key difference between our example and the stock market. With the stock market, instead of buying the share directly from the company, you often buy it from an existing investor. For instance, let's continue our snow cone example above and consider what happens if three days later, the sister needs money. She could ask her father if he would give her $10 for half of her share of the snow cone stand. Now, instead of the father buying his share directly from the snow cone business, he's purchasing it from an investor. The father agrees, happy to be a part of the new family business, and pays his daughter $10 for half her share of the company. Both the father and the daughter now own 12.5% of the snow cone stand.

Exhibit 31 – Four family members now have a share of the snow cone stand. The founding boy kept half of the business for his efforts in coordinating everything and running the stand.

Family Member	Founder	Brother	Sister	Father
Amount Invested	His time	$20	$10	$10
Ownership Share	50%	25%	12.5%	12.5%

Share Value

Shares are bought and sold—or traded—at whatever price the buyer and seller agree is fair. The value of a share depends on a great deal of factors that often involve uncertainty. As a result, everyone may have a different opinion of what a share is worth. It's only when two people agree to a price that a trade takes place. Once again revisiting our snow cone example, $20 for 25% ownership could be an excellent investment if the boy can generate large profits.

However, it's also possible that due to a lack of customers or an increase in the cost of syrup, the stand could lose money. As more information is learned about the snow cone stand's performance, the value of the shares could go up or down. For example, if two weeks in, the ambitious young boy has made $60, the value of the shares would be worth much more than before. However, if lower temperatures and rainfall prevent sales for a month, the value of the shares would likely fall.

There are two ways to make money in the stock market. You can purchase a share and keep it for many years, collecting your share of the company's profits as time passes, or you can purchase a share and sell it later for more than you originally paid. For example, if the brother who paid $20 for his 25% share later sells to his mother for $40, he'd earn a $20 profit.

Buying and holding or, buying and selling stocks offer the chance to grow your savings at a faster rate. It's important to once again mention that buying stocks—and many of the investment options we'll discuss—presents the potential that you'll lose money. If the father wants to sell his share after the stand has been struggling for a month, he may only get $5. As a result, the father has lost 50% of his money by purchasing the share for $10 and selling it for $5.

Historical Performance

There is a risk that if you buy stocks, you could lose some of your money. We mentioned briefly in Chapter 3 that the Canadian stock market lost roughly 14% in 2002 and 33% in 2008. However, we also mentioned that over ten-year periods average returns ranged from 3% to 11%. These numbers are based on the performance of a popular Canadian exchange-traded fund (ETF)—which we'll discuss in chapter 14—that invests in a broad range of Canadian companies.

Throughout history, investing in stocks over long periods has provided positive returns. These positive returns make sense when we once again consider what investing in stocks really is. You're buying partial ownership of a diverse range of companies. The goal for all these companies is to provide a product or service that's worth more to a customer than it costs to produce. While it isn't always the case, most companies succeed in creating value through their operations. The value created results in the stock market increasing in value over time.

Factors That Affect Share Value

Now that we understand how a share works, let's discuss the factors that drive what it's worth. Since a share is a portion of a company, its value depends on:

1. What the company **owns**, also called assets
   - This could include cash, buildings, patents, trademarks and more.
2. What the company **owes**, also called liabilities
   - This could include loans, amounts owed to suppliers and more.
3. What the company **earns**, also called net income
   - This includes current and future profits or losses.

Depending on the type of company, these factors will differ in importance. For instance, companies that operate in traditional industries, like manufacturing or real estate, may own a lot of buildings. In this case, the amount they own could be an important consideration. In a different case, a tech company may own little more than an app. Here, the share would be valued on how much the company could earn in the future. In either case, if a company owes a lot to borrowers, this can be the most important factor an investor considers.

You may not be interested in picking individual stocks, and for most of us, that's the right approach. However, understanding how the stock market works will help increase your comfort using it to help grow your savings. Let's continue discussing the factors that investors consider when deciding whether to buy or sell stocks.

Book Value

The simplest way to value a company is to look at what it owns and subtract what it owes. If a company owns its head office, factory and delivery trucks, they could have $200 million in assets. They may have borrowed $50 million from a bank and owe their suppliers $5 million for a recent delivery. In this case, if the company sold everything it owned and paid back what it owed, it would have $145 million left. This $145 million value is referred to as the company's book value. It's what the company's worth today if they sold everything and stopped operating.

When you invest in the stock market, you're buying companies that own assets like buildings and patents. These assets are what you see as you walk down the street or what you feel as you enter your favourite store. Either way, the value of a share is backed up partially by what the company owns.

Earnings

A company's goal is to use what they own to earn money by selling goods or services for more than they cost. Therefore, rather than simply considering the book value, most investors consider what the company can earn. Some companies are focused on earning a profit today, and others are willing to wait.

Companies can be categorized depending on what stage of growth they're at. Some may be growing their business for the future, while others are at a mature state with little room left to grow. When considering a growth company, its current earnings are less important than what it could earn in the future. An established company that's investing to grow additional services is considered both on its current and future earnings. Mature companies that aren't increasing capacity or entering new markets are valued based on current earnings.

Exhibit 32 – Companies can be categorized into three stages of growth. Depending on the company's stage, investors are focused on different types of earnings.

Category	Investor Focus
Growth	Potential future earnings
Established	Current and future earnings
Mature	Current earnings

Earnings are important because they allow the company to grow or pay you back money. A common approach to valuing a company is to forecast the amount it could earn over its lifetime. If a company could earn $10 billion over the next twenty years, it may be worth $5 billion today. It's worth less today than it may earn since that money is both uncertain and in the future.

Market Value

Investors consider what the company owns and owes, which is represented by the book value. They also look at the potential earnings of the company in the future. This combination allows them to determine what the company is worth today. The total value of the business based on what investors believe is referred to as its market capitalization. This is also referred to as market cap or market value, and it's what the market of investors believes the company is worth.

The market value is calculated by multiplying the number of shares in the company by the current price of a share. For instance, a company with 10 million shares and a $100 share price would have a market cap of $1 billion. Typically, companies are grouped by their market cap into small-cap (less than $2 billion), mid-cap (from $2 billion to $10 billion) and large-cap (larger than $10 billion). A company's market capitalization can influence who owns its shares and how easy its shares are to buy and sell.

Comparing the Price to Earnings

While a company's earnings are important, looking at them on their own doesn't help much. For instance, earnings of $50 million could be excellent for a small company with 100 employees or disaster for a global business. To address this, a commonly referenced measurement is a P/E ratio. This stands for price-to-earnings ratio, and it's a comparison of a company's earnings to its market cap. In our previous example, if a company had earnings of $50 million and was worth $1 billion, its P/E ratio would be twenty.

You can view the P/E ratio as how many years' profit the company needs to pay back your investment in full. If the company makes $50 million for twenty years, they'd have earned their current value of $1 billion. These numbers also give a sense of the return you're earning on your investment. If the company earns $50 million and is worth $1 billion, they're earning 5% a year.

P/E ratios vary over time, depending on economic conditions. However, the average is often between ten and twenty. High P/E ratios are very common for high-growth companies that expect larger earnings in the future. As the company's earnings increase and growth slows, the P/E ratio typically decreases. Low P/E ratios are common for stocks that are having difficulties and may earn less in the future. A P/E ratio is a quick way to compare two companies of similar size and stage of growth.

Exhibit 33 – Earnings are very important to a share's value. However, it needs to be compared to the size of the company. The following chart outlines a range of P/E ratios with examples.

Example	P/E	Reasoning
Historical average	10 to 20	Provides a return between 5% to 10%
Growing tech company	50	Future earnings are expected to be much higher
Established bank	14	Consistent earnings offering a return of 7%
Struggling global brand	8	Risk that earnings will soon fall

Dividends

Earnings allow companies to grow or give money back to their investors. One way they can give money back is by paying you a dividend. This is often done by more established companies that no longer need all their profit to grow. Dividends are the simplest way to see the return on your investment in a stock. For example, if you buy a share for $20 and each year you get $1 in dividends, your return from dividends is 5%. This 5% value is called the dividend yield. Dividend yields typically range from 1% to 10%, with an average around 2.5%. An important note is that companies can lower their dividend at any time. Therefore, just because a company is paying a high dividend today, doesn't mean they'll continue to. Companies try to avoid lowering their dividend, but in challenging times, it happens.

Emotions

We mentioned above that there are three main factors that determine what a share is worth.

1. What the company **owns**
2. What the company **owes**
3. What the company **earns**

However, there's a fourth factor that should be added to the list.

4. How investors **feel**
   - This could include hope, excitement, euphoria, anxiety, fear, panic and more.

As investors view the same share while in a different emotional state, the value can change dramatically. If you're excited for the future of an industry, like electric cars, you'll probably view these manufacturers more favourably. You may believe the company's future earnings will be enormous and will be prepared to pay more for a share. However, several months later, you may fear the economy is slowing down and that future earnings will be low. In this case, you may pay very little for the same share.

These emotions can swing from day to day, as well as in longer-term cycles. While very little may have changed for the company, the price of its shares can move up or down significantly. Regardless of the type of emotion, it's important to remember how much of a role they play in the stock market. This, once again, emphasizes the importance of ignoring the noise. Remember that underlying all your stock investments are assets and potential future earnings.

Exhibit 34 – Combining what the company owns, owes and earns determines what it's worth.

Exhibit 35 – Investors view this share over time while in different emotional states. In good times, they apply a premium and pay more, and in bad times, they apply a discount and pay less.

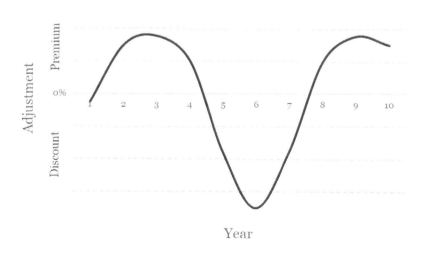

Exhibit 36 – The combination of all these factors creates the share price over time.

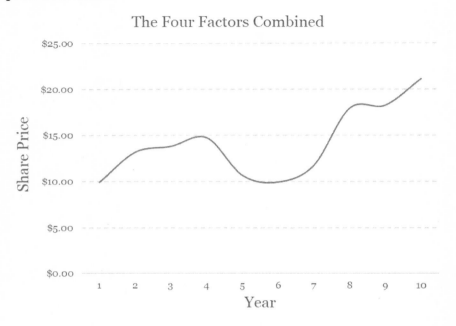

Managing Risk

A company's value is highly dependent on an uncertain future. If a change in regulation limits a factory's production, then its value falls. If a company loses a major client, it's future earnings could drop significantly. These events are unpredictable, which is why the stock market presents a higher level of risk. Layered on top of the risks to the business, there is also a risk that investor emotions will shift. All this risk is especially high if you buy only a few companies. If you invest 100% of your money in a single company and it loses a major lawsuit, you could lose everything. However, if you invest 1% of your money in 100 companies and any go bankrupt, you'd lose up to 1%. To lower the impact an event can have on your savings, it's wise to diversify.

Final Thoughts

As we mentioned in Chapter 4, it's common to invest in higher-risk investments to help earn a higher return. To do this, it's important that you don't need your money in the near-term. The stock market has historically been a way to put your money to work to grow your savings for the future. You can invest in stocks with savings in any of the accounts we discuss in this book. Regardless of the account, it's important to remember the material covered in part I. This includes your risk exposure, diversification, long-term investing, research and obtaining a professional opinion as required. With the stock market now covered, it's time to discuss lower-risk investment options. These options can provide greater diversity and predictability to your savings.

Key Takeaways

- Stocks are a common way to grow savings at a faster rate while taking on more risk.
- Minimize your risk by investing in many different companies over a long period.
- Stock prices are determined by what a company owns, owes and earns, as well as investors' emotions.

Chapter 13

Fixed Income

The stock market offers a way to potentially grow your savings at a faster rate. However, this option has higher risk, especially over a short period. Instead of, or in addition to, investing in stocks you can invest in a range of fixed income options. As the name would suggest, these investments are designed to provide a more fixed—or predictable—return. They tell you up front when and how you'll be paid back on your investment.

We mentioned in Chapter 3 that there are two main categories of investments. The first is to own, like buying a stock. The second is to lend, which is what you do with fixed income options. There are lots of fixed income options available, some of which you're likely already familiar with. A savings account that pays interest is the simplest form of fixed income. Your financial institution tells you that each day, you'll earn a fixed amount of interest. Another example is a guaranteed investment certificate (GIC). Financial institutions want to borrow money from you for fixed periods of time, often one to five years. If you buy a GIC, you're lending your money for that fixed period in exchange for interest. The final option we'll discuss is a bond.

In all these cases, the return is more predictable than higher-risk investments. If you have a long time before you need your money, you may only invest a small portion of your savings in fixed income. However, if you only have a few years to invest, or if you'd like to diversify, fixed income options are excellent.

Guaranteed Investment Certificates (GICs)

If you don't need your money for a year or more and don't want to invest in higher-risk options, GICs are a common choice. GICs typically require that you commit to lending your money for a fixed period. If you need your money back before the period is over, there can be penalties. Because you're agreeing to lend for a fixed period, the borrower is often willing to pay you a higher interest rate. For instance, the interest on a savings account where you can withdraw any time may be 1.5%. However, if you commit to lending for a year through buying a one-year GIC, you may receive 2% interest. In addition, typically the longer you lend your money, the higher your return. Instead of buying a one-year GIC and earning 2%, you could buy a three-year GIC and receive 2.5% a year.

In Canada, GICs are guaranteed by the financial institution you're buying from. In addition, if for any reason they can't pay you back, your money may also be protected by the CDIC. The Canada Deposit Insurance Corporation (CDIC) offers insurance up to a maximum of $100,000 for certain deposits. You can speak with your financial institution or CDIC to learn more about the coverage, given your situation. Because GICs define the rate of return and period up front, they're much more predictable than the stock market. However, the rate of return is likely to be lower than what has historically been earned in the stock market. Before purchasing a GIC, it's important to consider two things. Check if the return is higher than a savings account by enough to justify locking in your money. Confirm if you're in a position where you could take on more risk and potentially earn a higher return through a different option.

Bonds

Another fixed income investment option is a bond. Most people are unfamiliar with bonds, and it's unlikely you'll ever buy one directly. However, it's important to understand what they are and how they work. We've mentioned that for most people, an easy approach to investing is to buy a fund, which we'll cover in the next chapter. These funds typically buy bonds on your behalf for the fixed income portion of the investment.

Bonds are used by companies and governments to raise money needed to operate. The first step is for the company or government to issue the bond. This is the term used when the bond is first created. The bond is then exchanged for the loan payment from the investor. After the bond has been issued, it can be traded—or bought and sold—similarly to a share. The primary difference between a bond and a share is the amount of uncertainty to returns. As we covered previously, a share gives you ownership to a portion of a company, which has an uncertain future value. A bond, on the other hand, offers more certainty. You lend your money to a company or government today in exchange for repayment of your money plus interest in the future. The return in this case is better defined and equals the interest received over time.

Let's think back to our snow cone stand example and consider if the boy had taken a slightly different approach. Like before, the boy asks his siblings to borrow $20 from each of them to start his stand. However, instead of offering ownership—or shares—in his business, he decides to issue a bond to each of his siblings. In exchange for the $20 today, he guarantees them $2 at the end of each month for the next four months. He also promises to return their $20 in four months' time. In this case, the return on the siblings' money is clear to see. By lending $20 today, the siblings stand to make $8 in interest and receive their $20 back in four months. Therefore, provided the snow cone stand can make all the scheduled payments, the siblings will earn a profit of $8 each.

Rate of Return

The return on a bond is more predictable than a stock because the payments are defined ahead of time. Bonds still carry some risk. For instance, if the company or government can't make interest payments or return the loan, you could lose money. This can happen through poor management, unexpected economic conditions or a list of other reasons. The risk that the bond may not be repaid is what determines the return—or interest—that must be paid. The higher the risk the bond may not be paid back, the higher the return it should offer.

Bond Value

Just as the stock market offered the ability to trade shares, bonds can be purchased and sold in a similar manner. Like stocks, there are several factors used to determine the value of a bond. These include:

1. **How much** you'll be paid, also called interest rate
    - This is the amount of any interest payments received each year.
2. **When** you're paid back, also called maturity date
    - This is the date you receive your initial loan back.
3. **How likely** you'll be paid, also called bond rating
    - This includes receiving both the interest and repayment of the original loan.

Interest Rate

The interest rate—or coupon rate—is the amount of interest received each year. Bonds may offer interest payments ranging from 0% to 5%. You may be able to find higher interest rates, but these are typically paid by lower quality bonds. The interest payment a bond offers depends on the quality and length of the loan. The higher the interest rate—if everything else is the same—the more an investor is willing to pay for a bond.

Maturity Date

The maturity date of a bond is when you receive your original loan back. Bonds can be categorized as short-term (maturing in the next three years), medium-term (maturing in four to ten years) or long-term (maturing in greater than ten years). A longer maturity bond carries greater risk due to the uncertainty that you'll be repaid. In addition, committing to a longer period means you may miss out on other investment opportunities. As a result, long-term bonds usually offer a higher return than short-term bonds.

Bond Rating

The bond rating is the quality of the bond, or the chance that it will be repaid. The higher the quality, the lower the chance the company will default, or not pay back the loan. Bond ratings follow a grade system and range from AAA down to C or D. AAA are the highest quality—or safest—and C or D are referred to as junk bonds. These junk bonds have a higher uncertainty of repayment.

One of the main benefits of bonds is that they typically hold less risk than other investments like stocks. However, not all bonds offer this lower level of risk. Bonds that are rated below BBB are considered non-investment grade. These carry higher risk than investment grade bonds that range from AAA to BBB. As a result, it's important to avoid non-investment grade bonds when investing for the low-risk portion of a portfolio.

The higher the rating, the more an investor is willing to pay. If a company's bonds are downgraded from AA to A, the value of their bonds will decline. Because investors are willing to pay more for high-quality bonds, the return on these bonds is lower.

Bond Prices

Over time, like shares, bond prices fluctuate in value. Depending on the interest rate, maturity date and bond rating, a bond's price will change due to market developments. As interest rates of equal risk investments change, the prices of all existing bonds are impacted. If the interest rate offered on new bonds decreases, the attractiveness and price of current bonds increases. These existing bonds are locked in at a higher rate of return. Therefore, they're purchased until the expected return of all similar investments are the same. As interest rates increase, the opposite happens, and all existing bonds become less valuable. The longer the time until maturity, the more the bond price changes.

Diversification

Diversification, once again, plays an important role when purchasing bonds. To minimize the risk of losing money when buying bonds, it's important to invest in a diverse range of them. This can be done by purchasing bonds backed by different companies and governments. It can also help to buy some bonds that mature soon and others that mature in the future. For instance, the most recent economic crisis in 2008 was partially due to a specific type of bond. These bonds were mortgage-backed securities, meaning they were used to lend to people to buy houses. The bonds were incorrectly rated as high-quality investments. This error and the resulting losses in these bonds demonstrate that diversification continues to be critical, even with fixed income investments.

Investing part of your savings in bonds, or any fixed income, can be a great way to minimize your chance of loss. Throughout history, as stocks and other investments decline in value due to uncertainty, bonds typically rise in value. Investors move their money into safer investments in times of uncertainty, which increases the price of your bonds. This allows returns on bonds to offset losses on stocks, making your returns more consistent.

Final Thoughts

We've now seen that returns from bonds are much more structured. These returns can often be used as a type of consistent and dependable form of income. As retirement approaches, you can invest more money in fixed income investments. This will help cover various expenses throughout retirement. Instead of selling shares to generate money for groceries and other expenses, you can use interest payments. The lower-risk and predictable income make fixed income investments desirable in the later periods of a savings plan.

Key Takeaways

- Fixed income investments offer a more predictable way to grow your money, typically at a slower rate.
- Diversify your savings by investing in multiple fixed income options.
- Bond prices are determined by how much, when and how likely you'll be paid by the borrower.

Chapter 14

Investment Funds

Stocks and bonds provide the opportunity to grow your money through compounded returns. You could pick and choose individual companies if your interests and skillset permit. Or, a popular alternative is to purchase mutual funds or exchange-traded funds (ETFs). Because it's challenging to pick the best stock or bond, it can help to own a wide range of investments. This approach maximizes the chance you'll own a portion of the next breakthrough company.

Mutual funds and ETFs allow you to own a diverse range of shares and bonds with a single purchase. These simple and diversified funds help you benefit from compound growth while minimizing your workload and chance of loss. Rather than having to purchase and manage a long list of stocks and bonds, you can purchase a short list of mutual funds or ETFs. These funds then invest in a diverse range of shares or bonds for you.

Buying a Fund

You can invest in ETFs and mutual funds through most brokerage accounts. You can set up a brokerage account online with a wide range of providers, including most banks. There are differences in the fees you pay, ease of use and speed of transferring money to and from your account. You can find rankings of the top brokerages online. By researching the different companies that offer brokerage accounts, you'll find the one that's best for your needs.

You can also invest in mutual funds and ETFs in several other ways. Some options provide advice and help with financial planning, taxes and more. You'll pay higher fees for these options, but if your situation is more complex or you value the support, it can be worth it.

You can also purchase mutual funds directly from the company that manages the fund. Regardless of how you access these funds, they're an excellent way to simplify investing.

Investment Objective

Each fund has an investment objective that describes what they'll buy. There are funds that focus on stocks, funds that focus on bonds or those that invest in both. Some funds are split by global markets, such as Canada, U.S., Europe or developing countries. Fixed income funds can focus on corporate bonds or government bonds. They may also invest solely in short- or long-term bonds.

There are many different funds to meet a wide range of investor needs. If you're saving for two years, you may want a low-risk investment focused on Canadian bonds. In this case, you could buy a fixed income ETF that holds short-term bonds. If you're saving for retirement, you may invest in four or five different ETFs. This could include:

- An ETF that invests in Canadian stocks and bonds
- An ETF that invests in U.S. stocks and bonds
- A mutual fund that invests in European bonds
- An ETF that invests in stocks from developing countries

This demonstrates how you can diversify your investments with just a few funds. It's important not to invest just in Canada because we're only a small portion of the global economy.

Management Expense Ratio (MER)

Funds are either actively or passively managed. This difference is important because it often has a large impact on the fees you pay. The management expense ratio (MER) of the fund is one of the most important figures to consider. It's how much of your money is used on an annual basis to pay for the managing team's time, resources and expenses. The higher the MER, the more the managers of the fund are costing. Generally, higher MERs—usually greater than 1%— are associated with actively managed funds. These funds do research and regularly buy and sell new investments, experiencing high costs. Less expensive funds—usually with MERs of 0.5% or less—typically follow indexes or broad markets. These funds buy a pre-set list of investments instead of picking and choosing. Therefore, they need less research and trading, thereby lowering their costs.

Exhibit 37 – Funds can be categorized as being actively or passively managed. The approach has a major impact on the fees you pay.

Management	Description	Typical MER
Passive	Buy a pre-set list of investments, often referred to as an index	0.1% to 0.5%
Active	Buy and sell stocks based on research, trying to outperform the market	> 1%

How the MER Impacts Your Return

The MER of a fund is important because it's a cost that's independent of the fund's performance. Therefore, when the fund does well, the MER is deducted before the profits are passed on to you. When the fund does poorly, the MER is still deducted and causes an even larger loss. While 2% may not seem like a significant number, it's remarkable the impact this fee has on your savings. Another way to consider a 2% MER is to compare it to the total gains that are earned each year. If a fund earns 7% each year, then the fund has spent almost 1/3 of the profits on expenses to operate.

As we saw with companies in Chapter 12, creating value requires you produce something worth more than it costs. Therefore, a fund is only creating value if it can offset the 2% fee with higher returns on the investments it picks. There are various opinions on the benefits of an actively managed portfolio both for and against. So much of the stock market is unpredictable. Therefore, an argument against active management is that the benefits of additional research and speculation don't offset the costs.

While it may be possible to outperform the market for short periods of time, it's been very difficult over long periods. There are strong opinions and historical data to support that active management underperforms passive management after considering the higher fees.

An increasingly common approach is to use passive funds that invest in a broad range of companies. Most often, these funds follow an index. The index provides a list of investments determined by a committee or rule set. The goal is to represent a specific market, such as the Canadian or U.S. stock market. An example of an index is the S&P/TSX Composite Index. This is a list of roughly 250 companies that represent approximately 70% of the value of the Canadian stock market.

Another index is the S&P 500. It includes 500 large U.S. companies that are selected by a committee of market professionals. This index is intended to represent the U.S. economy. A fund that follows the S&P 500 can operate at a lower cost than an actively traded fund. This is because the list of companies to invest in is predefined, resulting in less research, trading and other costly activities. Investing in a selection of low MER funds will put more of your money toward earning a return instead of toward fees.

The following example demonstrates how MERs can have a significant impact on the growth of your savings. To achieve this, we'll compare the result of two savings plans invested in different funds. Both are invested in the Canadian stock market with the same performance of the investments in each fund. The only difference is that one fund will be charged a 1.5% MER, and the second will be charged a 0.25% MER. We'll assume the Canadian market increases by an average of 7% annually over a thirty-year period.

The first account that is paying 1.5% in fees receives returns of 5.5% a year. This is because the MER is subtracted from the market's performance. This account will grow from $10,000 to $49,800 over thirty years. The second account that is charged an MER of 0.25% would receive 6.75% growth after fees. The account would, therefore, increase from $10,000 to $71,000. This shows that even though the difference in MER is only 1.25%, the impact to your savings is a loss of 30%. This is because of compound interest, which we discussed in Chapter 2. Once again, this shows that small changes in your rate of return can have a huge impact over long periods of time.

Exhibit 38 – Saving just 1.25% in annual fees allows your account to grow an additional $21,100 over thirty years.

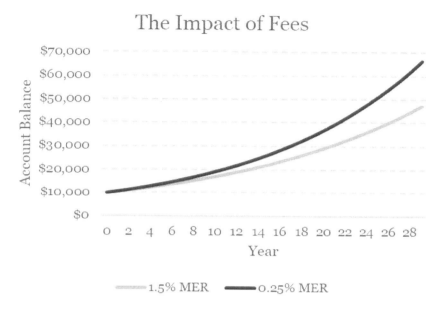

Other Factors to Consider

In addition to reviewing the MER of a given fund, it's important to consider the track record and any fine print. While historical performance doesn't guarantee future results, it shows if the fund can meet its investment objectives. Some mutual funds require minimum deposit lengths to avoid additional fees. Other funds have front- or back-end charges to invest in or withdraw money from the fund.

Final Thoughts

Mutual funds and ETFs offer a very simple way to invest. With the purchase of only a few funds, it's possible to own a diversified set of investments. Stocks and bonds from around the world are available with minimal effort. Mutual funds and ETFs offer the diversification and risk exposure that is so important to the success of your investments. They're also available without the hassle of purchasing and monitoring numerous individual investments. Through buying funds as you set aside savings, the task of investing for the future is made much easier.

Key Takeaways

- ETFs and mutual funds simplify investing by purchasing stocks and bonds for you.
- Minimizing the fees you pay will put more of your money to work for your future.
- A difference of just 1.25% in annual fees can lower your savings by 30%.

Chapter 15

Real Estate

One of the largest financial obligations in life is the task of providing shelter. Often, the first major decision in the process is whether to rent or buy. As we saw in Chapter 6 when we discussed budgeting, monthly costs for housing are a significant expense. Therefore, it's worth spending some time to consider the varying trade-offs involved. All too often, the debate of renting or buying comes down to what seems to be the simplest argument. One option offers no return, and the other offers the opportunity to build wealth. While this is an important piece of the decision, it's an oversimplification. Buying and renting both offer pros and cons that need to be considered to decide what's best for your financial situation.

Home Ownership

Buying a home allows your monthly mortgage payments to go toward building ownership. This gradually increases your net worth and, over time, builds financial security. In addition, once your mortgage is paid off, your monthly costs drop dramatically. Home ownership also provides peace of mind because there's less of a risk that you'll be required to move unexpectedly. For many, it also provides a sense of accomplishment.

While there's plenty of pros for home ownership, there are also several cons. There are additional costs and risks that come along with buying an immobile and deteriorating property. The transaction costs when buying and selling a home can be quite substantial. Therefore, buying a home is often only beneficial if you plan to own it for a lengthy period. Buying property may limit your ability to move if a job opportunity or personal emergency were to require it. Additionally, ongoing upkeep of a home can sometimes result in large, unexpected expenses. For example, the cost to replace a water heater or repair a roof can be substantial, and the timing can be unpredictable. Having a rainy day fund can help in these situations, but risk remains.

Renting

The aspects that make owning a home risky are the same that make renting desirable. With a rental agreement, your commitment is typically quite short, often a year's lease followed by sixty days' notice. This ability to come and go as you need is very valuable for anyone with an uncertain future. The risk of anything in the property needing repair falls on the owner. While rent payments aren't going toward building your net worth, they allow for mobility and prevent unexpected expenses. Too often, rent is considered throwing away your money. Instead, rent should be looked at just as any other product or service you buy. You're paying for a place to live while you study or work, with flexibility to move and predictability of expenses.

Comparing the Pros and Cons

Deciding between renting and buying is an important choice with implications that could last decades. By weighing your options and running best- and worst-case scenarios, you can decide confidently what's best for your needs. To demonstrate this decision process, we'll observe a young married couple as they consider buying a home near downtown Toronto. There's a lengthy list of possible considerations when deciding between renting and buying. Costs, square footage, location, your comfort with risk and certainty of the future are a small sample. To start, we'll focus on the first topic of costs.

Comparing Costs

The married couple in our example is looking to buy a home with a budget of $700,000. They plan to provide 20% as a down payment to avoid needing mortgage insurance. In addition to their down payment of $140,000, they'll need a mortgage of $560,000. They plan to pay off the mortgage over twenty-five years and pay an annual interest rate of 4%. The resulting monthly mortgage payment is $2,940. In addition, the couple will need to pay closing costs of roughly $28,000. This is 4% of the purchase price and includes land transfer tax, insurance and other one-time costs. An important note is that first-time home buyers can qualify for certain refunds. For instance, a land transfer tax refund is available given certain conditions are met. Another possibility is the First-Time Home Buyers' (FTHB) tax credit. As a result, it's possible to lower the up-front costs in certain cases.

Beyond up-front costs, the couple will need to budget for ongoing costs in addition to the mortgage. These include maintenance, property tax, insurance, utilities and more. Residential property taxes in Toronto are roughly 0.6% a year, or $4,200 on a $700,000 house. An annual maintenance budget could be 1%, or $7,000. We'll assume the remaining costs are roughly $300 a month. The result is an average monthly expense of $1,230 on top of the mortgage cost.

Exhibit 39 – Costs of home ownership include both up-front costs and ongoing monthly costs.

Up-front Costs		Monthly Costs	
Down payment	$140,000	Mortgage	$2,940
Closing costs	$28,000	Other	$1,230
Total	**$168,000**	Total	**$4,170**

With a better idea of the up-front and ongoing costs of buying a home, the couple can decide if it's right for them. Currently, the couple has a rental unit costing them $2,600 a month, including insurance and utilities. The additional monthly costs of $1,570 for home ownership is a substantial change to their cash flow. In addition, if the couple continues to rent, they can invest their money and allow it to grow. The level of risk the couple can take on the investment depends on how long they're comfortable waiting before they buy. If they'd like to reassess in a year, their money may be best in low-risk investments, like a savings account or GIC. With more time, they could take on more risk and potentially grow their savings at a faster rate.

Other Factors to Consider

From an initial comparison of the costs, the decision is expanded to the other factors we mentioned earlier. These included square footage, location, comfort with risk and certainty of the future. If they need the additional room to start a family, then there's value in making the move. However, if it's farther away from work and friends, it could result in additional time and costs commuting. Some people view home ownership as a major goal in life and place higher value on it than others. There's risk both for and against buying property, and you'll need to determine which is more important to you.

If you buy a property and then interest rates increase, your monthly costs could go up. However, if you continue to rent and house prices where you want to live rise, you may not be able to afford your ideal home in the future. Once you know where you want to live and how much you can comfortably afford, you can decide whether to buy or rent. As your needs change, you can continue to reassess and see if a switch from one to the other may be suitable.

Investing in Real Estate

In addition to real estate you live in yourself, a common investment is owning real estate that other people use. We've now seen the advantages and disadvantages of renting and buying your home. The flexibility to move as you please and the predictability of not needing to make repairs are very valuable. Providing this value to others presents the opportunity to make a return on an investment in real estate. People are willing to pay you rent for the freedom it provides.

The risks associated with owning real estate are very similar to the risks stocks and bonds carry. There's a chance you'll earn less on your investment than you expect, and in the worst-case scenario, you could lose money. By taking on this risk and owning real estate, it's often possible to earn returns over long enough periods. Often, the increase in value of the property plus the rent charged is greater than the costs. These costs include interest on the mortgage, maintenance, taxes and insurance.

Exhibit 40 – You can earn a positive return through a real estate investment if the following formula holds true. The change in value of the property plus the rent received must be greater than the costs.

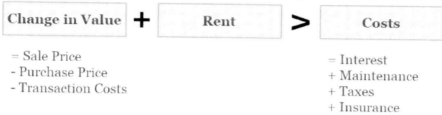

Change in Value	+	Rent	>	Costs

= Sale Price
- Purchase Price
- Transaction Costs

= Interest
+ Maintenance
+ Taxes
+ Insurance

Buying an Investment Property

Let's consider a simplified example of real estate being used as an investment to grow existing savings. A home within walking distance to a university is available on the market for $400,000. An initial investment of $80,000 would provide a 20% down payment to purchase the home. Assuming a mortgage at 5% paid over thirty years, the monthly mortgage payment would be $1,700. The house currently has tenants paying $2,400 a month in rent. Provided that the house remains occupied, the excess of $700 a month can go toward maintenance, insurance, taxes and various other expenses.

In addition to any remaining rent income at the end of each month, the mortgage payments are gradually paying back the loan. With every passing payment, the portion of the home owned by the investor continues to increase. In addition, there's the possibility that the value of the property will increase with time. Gradually, these can add up to offer a return on the initial $80,000 investment. The amount of the return can vary greatly and depends on a wide range of inputs, including:

- the percentage of time the property is occupied
- the cost of mortgage payments and other expenses
- the amount of rent being charged
- the amount the property is changing in value

Buying a Real Estate Investment Trust (REIT)

Real estate investments are popular partly because they offer two attractive features. They're something you can see, feel and easily understand, and they offer income from the rent payments over time. An alternative to buying a single investment property yourself is to buy partial ownership of a group of properties. Like buying a stock, you can buy units of a real estate investment trust (REIT). With this option, you can diversify your investment by owning a small part of many properties. It also removes the requirement to manage the property and find tenants, as this is handled by the trust.

Final Thoughts

Investing in real estate offers another way to diversify your savings. Often, people assume that history will repeat itself, and while it may, there's no guarantee. Property values in Canada have increased in value substantially and consistently throughout recent history. However, there's no guarantee this will continue. When buying a property to live in yourself or as an investment, ensure you've done your research. Your decision should be made for the right reasons, and you should consider both the best- and worst-case scenarios.

Key Takeaways

- Consider costs, your needs, your comfort with risk and more when deciding to rent or buy.
- Investing in real estate offers another way to diversify your savings.
- Assuming house prices will continue to rise is risky. Before you buy, consider the case where prices fall.

Chapter 16

The Registered Education Savings Plan (RESP)

Attending post-secondary school is becoming more common each year. Similarly, the costs of an education are increasing. To finance further schooling, many are relying on support from family or student loans. The cost of repaying student loans can challenge the financial well-being of a new grad. This can cause unwanted pressure to pursue a career that may provide immediately without offering future growth. As a result, any savings provided by family to pay for post-secondary education are very valuable.

A Registered Education Savings Plan (RESP) is, in most cases, the best way to do just this. The account allows you to make the most of any money put aside for a loved one's post-secondary education. In the simplest of RESP accounts, there are two people to consider: the creator of the account, called the subscriber, and the person the account is for, called the beneficiary. For example, if you're opening an account for your child's education, you'd be the subscriber and your child would be the beneficiary. The first step is for you, the subscriber, to open the account and start making deposits.

There are several RESP options available depending on your needs. For instance, joint accounts allow for multiple subscribers, so you and a spouse could deposit. In addition, there's family or group accounts that allow for multiple beneficiaries. Depending on your plans for the account and personal situation, there can be minor advantages to each account type. However, for our purposes, we'll focus on an individual account with one subscriber and one beneficiary.

RESP Benefits

There are two main attractions to the RESP that make it such a great savings product for education purposes. The first is that money grows tax free while it remains in the account. The second is the government grant and incentive programs that deposit additional money in the account.

Tax-Free Growth

Because money in an RESP grows tax free, it compounds at a faster rate. Then, once the growth is withdrawn, it's typically taxed at a low rate, if at all. In most cases, the withdrawal is referred to as an Educational Assistance Payment (EAP). These are withdrawals made to help the beneficiary pay for school. They're classified as income to the beneficiary. In most cases, the beneficiary has limited income while in school and, therefore, pays little if any tax on the withdrawals.

Government Incentives

In addition to tax-free growth, there are several grants and incentives offered by federal and provincial governments. Some of these grants are available to everyone, while others are only available to lower-income families. For simplicity, we'll focus on the two primary incentives that are offered by the federal government.

The Canada Education Savings Grant (CESG)

The first grant we'll discuss is the Canada Education Savings Grant (CESG). It matches 20% of your deposits to an RESP. Like the RRSP and TFSA, there are rules around when and how much you can contribute to the account. These include:

- The beneficiary accumulates $500 in potential grant matching each year.
- The grant will pay a maximum of $1,000 to the account in any one year.
- The grant will pay a maximum of $7,200 to the beneficiary in total.
- The maximum you can contribute to the account is $50,000.

Like employer retirement plans in Chapter 11, the accelerating power of matching is hard to pass up. By making a deposit to the RESP, you receive an immediate return of 20%. This is the equivalent of three years' growth at 6%.

In 2005, the CESG was expanded through the introduction of the Additional CESG. This was done to help middle- and low-income families reach their education savings goals more easily. The Additional CESG provides an extra 10% or 20% matching of the first $500 in contributions each year. Therefore, a qualifying beneficiary could receive an additional $100 a year deposited to their account. The Additional CESG counts toward the beneficiary's total lifetime limit of $7,200.

The Canada Learning Bond (CLB)

The second incentive is the Canada Learning Bond (CLB). It provides up to $2,000 for qualifying beneficiaries without requiring any contributions to the RESP. As a result, opening an RESP for a qualifying beneficiary can provide financial support without any obligation on the subscriber.

The CLB is slightly different than the CESG since it doesn't require any contributions to the RESP. Instead, it has other qualifying rules. To be eligible, the beneficiary must:

- be from a low-income household
- have been born on or after January 1, 2004
- be a resident of Canada
- have a valid SIN
- be named on an RESP

The first year they're eligible, the beneficiary receives $500 to the account. They also receive $100 each additional year they qualify, up to and including the year they turn fifteen. Therefore, a beneficiary that receives $500 the first year and $100 for the next fifteen years would receive the full $2,000.

Using the Account

The following example focuses on the two most common benefits of the RESP, the CESG and tax-deferred growth. A mother opens an

RESP for her two-year-old daughter. Each year since birth, her daughter has accumulated $500 in potential grant matching, even though she didn't have an account. Therefore, the daughter has a total of $1,500 in potential matching when the account is opened. The mother starts off with an initial deposit of $2,000. This deposit is met with a 20% match of $400 by the CESG.

Every year from her daughter's third to seventeenth birthday, the mother contributes $1,000 to the RESP. Each contribution is matched with a $200 grant. Assuming an annual return of 5% for fifteen years, the account would reach a value of $30,900. The balance of the account would be $17,000 in contributions from the mother, $3,400 in CESG and $10,500 in growth. The two main benefits of the RESP are the $3,400 in grants and $10,500 in growth, which has compounded tax free so far.

RESP Withdrawals

With an RESP created and funded, it's time to see how money is withdrawn. Since contributions to the RESP have already been taxed, they're not taxed when withdrawn. These contributions can be paid to either the beneficiary or subscriber. If the beneficiary is attending a qualifying or specified educational program, these withdrawals don't impact grants. In this case, a Post-Secondary Education (PSE) withdrawal is made. Both the grants and earnings collected throughout the life of the account can be withdrawn as EAPs. As we mentioned, these are taxable income to the beneficiary in the year they're withdrawn. In our previous example, the contributions totaled $17,000 and could be withdrawn with no taxes. Meanwhile, the $3,400 plus the $10,500 would be withdrawn as EAPs and taxable to the beneficiary.

Exhibit 41 – If the beneficiary attends a qualifying or specified educational program, the following flow of money applies.

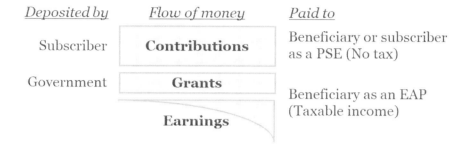

Deposited by	*Flow of money*	*Paid to*
Subscriber	**Contributions**	Beneficiary or subscriber as a PSE (No tax)
Government	**Grants**	Beneficiary as an EAP (Taxable income)
	Earnings	

Without Post-Secondary School

The intention of the RESP is for the money to help the beneficiary attend a post-secondary education. However, if the beneficiary doesn't pursue this route, there are still benefits to the RESP. The CESG contributions may be rolled over to a sibling in certain situations. Otherwise, these must be returned to the government since they were intended to pay for schooling. Your contributions can be withdrawn tax free. Any growth in the account, called Accumulated Income Payment (AIP), may be handled in one of two ways. Once certain requirements have been met, the AIP can be withdrawn and taxed as income plus an additional 20% tax. Or, again, provided certain conditions are met, the AIP can be rolled into an RRSP account.

Final Thoughts

The benefits of contributing to an RESP for education savings are substantial. The rules for contributing to an RESP and the grants you may qualify for may change over time. Additional information on opening, funding and using an account can be found online. You can find it on the Government of Canada's website or through any local financial institution that offers RESP accounts.

Key Takeaways

- Grant matching on deposits and tax advantages help your money for post-secondary schooling go further.

- You may qualify to receive money from the government without having to make deposits yourself.
- Complexities of the RESP make it worth learning more when you're ready to use the account.

Chapter 17

Taxes

You may have noticed by this point that the topic of taxes is mentioned a lot in this book. In fact, we've used the word tax over 150 times. This is because taxes are complicated in Canada, as in most of the world. After all, they've been built over decades to meet different goals along the way.

Most of the discussion has been about how to pay less tax. You can open a TFSA and avoid paying taxes on the growth of your investments. You can deposit money in an RRSP and avoid paying income tax until you withdraw. Or you can apply for tax credits when you buy your first home. Before we move on and learn more about how to pay less tax, let's first discuss why taxes are important.

Rationale for Taxes

Paying for goods and services individually, like we do for a car or movie, doesn't always make sense. For instance, splitting up the cost of a road or park between the people who use it is cumbersome and costly. It's also challenging to charge directly for services that police officers and firefighters provide. In addition, there are those who can't afford certain goods and services in their current situation and require support.

For these reasons and more, we've decided governments in Canada should provide certain services for us. From roads to education to health care, the government funds critical spending to help improve the standard of living of Canadians. To raise money for this spending, the various levels of government collect taxes. Paying these taxes can sometimes feel onerous and unwarranted because we don't see the benefit as we're paying. If you consider your childhood education, the local park you walk through on the weekend or visits to your doctor, paying tax is more bearable.

Why Taxes Are Complicated

Governments in Canada raise money through a range of taxes. You likely pay sales tax, income tax, payroll tax and property tax. These are collected by your municipal government, a provincial or territorial government or the federal government.

Three layers of government using different taxes to raise money provides enough complexity as it is. However, taxes are also used to incentivize desired behaviour. As we mentioned in Chapter 9, the government recognizes the value of your saving for retirement. If you save for later, you'll be less dependent on government services in retirement. As a result, to incentivize you to save, they created accounts like the TFSA and RRSP. They also see the value of saving for your child's education, so the next generation is well-trained and able to pay future taxes. Therefore, they created the RESP to help you save the money needed for post-secondary school.

In addition to saving for the future, governments provide tax breaks for a list of other activities, including:

- Donating to charity
- Purchasing your first home
- Furthering your education
- Having a child

Paying taxes is a matter of balancing the need for government spending with the value of the money if you get to keep it. We'll now cover the different types of taxes and ways to minimize what you pay using the incentives available to you.

Sales Tax

The most common tax you likely encounter is sales tax charged on individual purchases. While this is the most common tax, it's also one of the simplest and offers few ways to pay less of it. Therefore, you'll need to factor it into your savings plans when making large purchases. From cars to new construction homes, paying sales tax on a major expense can add thousands in unforeseen costs. While rare, there are some cases where you can receive rebates for sales tax paid. Examples include:

- GST/HST credit for low- to modest-income families
- GST/HST new housing rebate if you buy a new property

Income Tax

While you may only deal with income tax on an annual basis, it's a much larger tax than the others. For the year ended March 31, 2018, personal income tax accounted for 49% of the Government of Canada's revenues compared to 11.7% for GST. As a result, much of the opportunity to lower your taxes focuses on personal income tax.

You pay income tax to the federal government and your provincial or territorial government throughout the year. This is often done through direct payroll deductions that are sent to the CRA by your employer on your behalf. You then file your taxes annually to see whether the amount paid was the right amount. The deadline to file your income tax return is typically April 30. There are several key rules to paying income tax that are important to understand before we move on to ways to lower your taxes.

Tax Brackets

In Canada, as you earn more money in a year, you pay a higher percentage of your income to the government. This is the result of tax brackets that apply higher tax rates to higher levels of income. For instance, in British Columbia, income under $40,000 is charged a 20% tax, while income over $200,000 is charged roughly 50%. The exact amount you pay depends on your province or territory. However, the rates and process are similar across the country.

Exhibit 42 – The following tables show the federal tax rates and provincial tax rates for British Columbia as of 2019.

Federal	
Income	**Tax Rate**
first $47,630	15%
over $47,630 up to $95,259	20.5%
over $95,259 up to $147,667	26%
over $147,667 up to $210,371	29%
over $210,371	33%

British Columbia	
Income	**Tax Rate**
first $40,707	5.06%
over $40,707 up to $81,416	7.7%
over $81,416 up to $93,476	10.5%
over $93,476 up to $113,506	12.29%
over $113,506 up to $153,900	14.7%
over $153,900	16.8%

Exhibit 43 – By combining the federal and provincial rates, you get the total tax rate at each income bracket.

Federal and B.C. Combined	
Income	**Tax Rate**
first $40,707	20.06%
over $40,707 up to $47,630	22.7%
over $47,630 up to $81,416	28.2%
over $81,416 up to $93,476	31%
over $93,476 up to $95,259	32.79%
over $95,259 up to $113,506	38.29%
over $113,506 up to $147,667	40.7%
over $147,667 up to $153,900	43.7%
over $153,900 up to $210,371	45.8%
over $210,371	49.8%

This demonstrates that as your income increases, you pay a higher percent in taxes. If you earned $70,000 in British Columbia in 2019, you'd pay 20.06% on the first $40,707. You'd then pay 22.7% on the next $6,923 in earnings and 28.2% on the remaining $22,370. In total, you'd owe $16,045 in taxes.

There are two important income tax rates to consider:

1. Average income tax rate: the total tax you pay divided by your income. In the example above, the average tax rate is 23%, which is $16,045 divided by $70,000.
2. Marginal income tax rate: the rate you paid on the last dollar you earned. In the example above, the marginal tax rate is 28.2%, which was charged on the last $22,370 of income.

Exhibit 44 – With an income of $70,000 in British Columbia, the average income tax rate is 23% and the marginal rate is 28.2%.

Income	Tax Rate	
first $40,707	20.06%	
next $6,923	22.7%	Average = 23% Marginal = 28.2%
remaining $22,370	28.2%	

Non-Refundable Tax Credits

Non-refundable tax credits can help you lower your taxes owed each year. The most common credit is the basic personal amount, which lowers your federal income tax owed by $1,810 as of 2019. You can also lower your provincial or territorial income tax through this credit. There are additional non-refundable tax credits available in various situations. This may apply to you if you have dependents, are over the age of sixty-five, receive a pension, have a disability or meet other criteria.

Most tax software will help you determine the amount of taxes you owe and help you see which credits apply. If your situation is more complex, it may be worth speaking with a tax professional to ensure you're receiving the benefits intended.

Taxes on Your Investments

In addition to paying income tax on your salary, you also pay taxes on income from your investments. Growth on your investments may come from:

- Interest paid by a financial institution or bond issuer
- Dividends paid by a company
- Capital gains from selling an investment for more than you paid

Each type of income is taxed differently, as we'll see shortly. The opportunities to lower your taxes discussed in this book mostly apply to taxes on investment income.

Exhibit 45 – The following tax rules apply to the different types of investment income.

Income	Tax Rule
Interest	Taxed as regular income and added to your total for the year
Dividend	If paid by a Canadian company eligible for the dividend tax credit a lower rate is charged, otherwise taxed as regular income and added to your total for the year
Capital gain	50% of the gain is taxed as regular income and added to your total for the year

An important note is that investments held in a TFSA, RRSP or other registered account aren't charged these taxes. This is the main advantage of these accounts, since it simplifies your tax reporting and lowers what you owe. However, if you receive this income in a non-registered account, it's taxed at the appropriate rate. If you earned $70,000 in salary and received $5,000 of interest in a year, you'd pay tax as if you had income of $75,000. However, if you had a capital gain of $5,000, only half is added to your income, resulting in a total of $72,500. The number of accounts available and different rates charged on investment income results in a complex situation. As a result, you can benefit significantly by spending time to learn or work with a professional on where to put your money.

Payroll Tax

In addition to paying income tax on your salary, you're also charged other payroll taxes. These taxes fund the Canada Pension Plan (CPP) and Employment Insurance (EI). Each year, you're required to pay a portion of your earnings to the government up to a maximum amount. As of 2019, you're required to pay 5.1% of your earnings up to a maximum tax of $2,748.90 for CPP. In addition, you're charged 1.62% up to a maximum of $860.22 for EI. This additional $3,600 provides you with pension income in retirement, employment insurance and other benefits.

The CPP helps the government ensure Canadians have a base level of income in retirement. For those currently retired who qualify, the CPP provides income each year. The maximum annual payment is roughly $14,000, and the average amount paid is roughly $8,000 as of 2019. The amount you receive depends on the number of years you contribute to the CPP, the amount you contribute and when you choose to start receiving payments.

Property Tax

In Chapter 15, we watched a couple decide whether to continue renting or buy a new home. One cost involved in the decision was the property tax charged each year on the home. Property taxes are paid to your municipal government to provide many services. These vary by region and include items like parks, libraries, policing and snow removal. Property tax is charged based on your municipality and the value of your house. In the case of the couple in Chapter 15, the residential property tax in Toronto was roughly 0.6% a year. This resulted in an annual tax of $4,200 on a $700,000 property. Depending on your province and situation, you may receive tax credits for property taxes paid in certain cases.

Filing Your Taxes

As we mentioned above, you pay income taxes throughout the year and then file your taxes by April 30. Filing your taxes requires that you provide relevant data to the CRA, so they can determine if you owe additional taxes. You can obtain the information you need from various forms received around tax time. These can include information about:

- Income received from your employer
- Donation receipts
- RRSP contribution receipts
- Tuition payments
- Income received from investments

By combining all your income and any adjustments required, you'll know whether you owe the CRA or if you're owed a rebate.

If you're owed a rebate, it means that you've paid more in taxes throughout the year than you needed to. Rebates are often celebrated, as the money can be used for savings or other expenses. However, it also means you may be able to pay less in taxes throughout the year and can start using that extra money earlier.

There are several low-cost or free filing options available if your tax situation is simple. If your situation is more complex, you can meet with a tax expert to review your circumstances and help you file.

Other Ways to Lower Your Taxes

When you're filing your taxes, there are several other ways to lower your taxes. You can receive tax credits for a range of activities, some of which include:

- Interest paid on qualifying student loans
- Donations made to qualifying organizations
- Tuition paid to a qualifying institution
- Qualifying medical expenses
- Childcare expenses

There are many other potential ways to lower the amount of taxes you're required to pay. Some may not justify the additional work to document and track, while others can offer major savings. As we'll cover in Chapter 19, there are many resources available for you to learn more about taxes. It's something you'll likely need to do each year for the foreseeable future and is worth taking the time to understand.

Final Thoughts

The goal of this chapter is to cover the importance of taxes while explaining steps you can take to lower them. It's in your best interest, as well as Canada's best interest, for you to take advantage of the incentives available to you today. This helps the policies that are in place have the intended outcome. Therefore, it's worth taking the time to learn more about taxes or to work with a professional as needed. By using accounts like the RRSP and TFSA and claiming credits you're eligible for, you'll have more money available for your goals.

Key Takeaways

- Sales tax, income tax, payroll tax and property tax are paid to different levels of government in Canada.
- Reduce the amount of tax you pay by using registered accounts and claiming eligible credits.
- Continue to learn about taxes to take advantage of all the incentives, or work with a professional as required.

Summary II

As with the accessories added to a snowman, you could choose to go out to the store and purchase everything you need. You could also choose to do it yourself by crafting material found around the yard or house into suitable fittings. The same applies to the topics covered in part II. You can pay fees to advisors and fund managers who will help to increase the quality of your overall portfolio. The downside to this option is the costs that decrease the amount of money you have remaining to invest. You may not have the desire or ability to do everything yourself. However, the less you pay in fees, the more you can put toward your goals.

The accessories we've covered can be added to the foundation discussed in part I of this book. Getting to your money first and setting aside savings is easier if you've lowered your expenses and set up a budget. Maximizing your expected growth rate is possible through investing in stocks in a registered account, like the TFSA or RRSP.

A Financial Roadmap

To help see how these topics can come together, we'll observe Sam as he progresses with his finances over time:

1. For savings up until Sam turns eighteen, he uses a high-interest savings account from a local financial institution.
2. Once of age, he opens a TFSA and transfers his money into the account to avoid taxes going forward.
3. Since Sam's not ready to invest on a long-term basis, he still uses a high-interest savings product in his TFSA.
4. At the same time, he opens a student credit card to begin building credit and only spends money he already has.
5. As Sam starts his career, he sets up an automatic transfer into his savings account after each paycheque.

6. When he receives his first raise, he increases his transfer to his savings account before increasing his spending.
7. He begins investing his money in his TFSA for longer-term goals, such as buying a house and retirement.
8. He chooses a few low-cost funds to minimize the fees he's paying while taking on an appropriate amount of risk.
9. Sam switches jobs to an employer that offers a retirement plan and contributes the required amount to max out the matching.
10. Due to higher income and minimal room left to contribute to his TFSA, Sam opens an RRSP and starts depositing.
11. After years of saving for a down payment, he decides to buy a house after a careful assessment of the pros and cons.
12. He uses money from his RRSP through the HBP and takes advantage of several tax breaks for first-time home buyers.
13. With the purchase of a new house and a child shortly after, Sam buys insurance to protect against the unknown.
14. He also sets up a will to oversee his estate if he passes away.
15. To help provide education savings for his child, Sam opens an RESP and starts setting aside money early.
16. As Sam's retirement approaches, he sells some of his stocks, buys more fixed income and eventually switches his RRSP to a RRIF.

The accessories mentioned in part II may not be relevant for your immediate needs. Now that you have a foundational understanding of them, you can return to this section in the future. From time to time, it's worth checking back to see if there are new opportunities to expand your financial plan. For ease of future reference, the following table outlines the accessories discussed and key takeaways for each.

Accessory	Takeaway
Expenses	Rethink your expenses to identify where you get the most value and what you spend out of habit rather than intentionally
Budgeting	Spend your money on what's most important to you and work your way down the list until it's all assigned
Credit score	Start building your credit history early and be careful not to miss payments
Borrowing	Avoid high-interest loans and long payback periods to minimize the amount of your money going to someone else's savings
Insurance	Ensure you have appropriate coverage when you have dependents and buy expensive assets
Will	Create a will as major life events call for it and keep it up to date to ensure your estate is handled how you'd like
RRSP	Useful for retirement savings when you're in a high-income tax bracket or for special circumstances like the HBP or LLP
TFSA	Versatile for any savings goal to allow your money to grow tax free
Employer plan	Maximize contributions to any employer retirement plan if you receive matching deposits
Stock market	Owning stocks can help your money grow overtime, but year to year returns are unpredictable and sometimes negative
Fixed income	Lending money can provide a more predictable return on your savings and helps diversify your investments
Investment funds	Purchasing a fund that bundles investments together provides diversification with minimal effort and cost
Real estate	Buying property—whether to live in or rent out—is a major decision involving tradeoffs of predictability and flexibility
RESP	Take advantage of government grants and tax deferred growth when saving for any loved one's post-secondary education
Taxes	Minimize the amount of tax you pay by taking advantage of the incentives the government has created for you

The topics we've covered range from a ten-year-old saving some of their part-time income to someone entering retirement. You can add the accessories that apply to your current situation and expand your plan over time. With a strong grasp of personal finance in hand, it's time to move on to the final part of the book to see what's next from here.

Part III:
A Helping Hand

Building a snowman is rarely an endeavour taken on by a single person. You may work with friends and family at home or classmates in the school yard. Either way, the lengthy task of building a snowman becomes less intimidating as the work is shared with others. Beyond finding friends to help, sometimes tools, such as shovels, buckets and even a cup of water, can be used.

As with building a snowman, there are numerous resources available to assist you with managing your money. Since each financial situation differs, it's difficult to address every circumstance you may face in a single book. The good news is that with some additional research and learning, you can handle any situation you may come across.

There are numerous books, websites and video series that cover personal finance topics to expand your knowledge base. The following section will outline some of these resources and provide important things to consider along the way. We'll cover topics including:

- Your subconscious mind and how it's constantly working against your best intentions
- Important things to consider when reading through facts, opinions and suggestions
- Programs you can use to keep track of your finances

Whether it's a useful tool or help from a friend, you'll be ready for your future and can enjoy the journey along the way.

Chapter 18

Your Subconscious Mind

Everything we've covered so far has helped your conscious mind better understand how to manage your money. You know the importance of starting early, the power of compound growth and the dangers of borrowing. However, unless you take specific steps, which we'll cover shortly, you're unlikely to reach your goals. This is because your conscious mind has little to do with your day-to-day decisions. Your spending habits form over time and then happen subconsciously, with little further thought. In the opening of this book, I mentioned that one of the greatest challenges with personal finance is that we're wired to be bad at it.

As a species, we've only been saving and investing for a short period of our existence. Saving for the future seems a lot less important if you don't know if you'll make it back to the cave alive at the end of a hunt. Over time, our subconscious mind built up a series of simplifications or shortcuts to make decisions easier and faster. Errors caused by these shortcuts are called cognitive biases. Most of the time, these biases aren't an issue, and you're still better off using the shortcuts, since they allow you to avoid thinking through every decision. However, when it comes to managing your money, these biases make your job much harder than it needs to be.

Hyperbolic Discounting

Delayed gratification requires putting off an immediate reward today in exchange for a greater reward in the future. This is a critical skill to develop both in life and for your financial success. However, this is more easily said than done. Setting aside money for the future is so hard because there's such a salient benefit to spend it today.

Meanwhile, the benefit of putting it aside for later is unclear. The challenge to delay gratification can be explained by a behavioural bias referred to as hyperbolic discounting. This bias applies an unreasonably high discount to rewards in the future.

Exhibit 46 – The following chart is an illustrative example of how your mind values a cookie depending on when it's received.

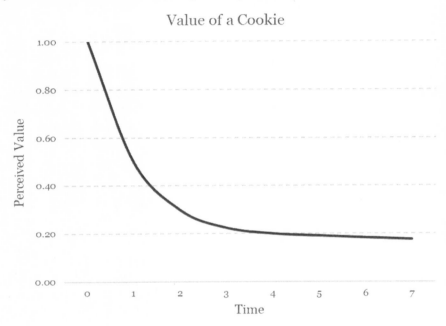

The most important thing to observe is how quickly the perceived value drops. A reward today is much preferred to one tomorrow. However, this preference quickly slows, and a reward in a month isn't much better than a reward in ten years. Knowing that you're wired to act this way is an important step in taking control of your money.

Automate Your Savings

To mitigate the impact of hyperbolic discounting on your success, you can automate your savings. This removes the real-time decisions when you're most likely to favour a reward today. As we mentioned in Chapter 1, you can set up an automatic transfer from your chequing account to your savings account. This can be done right as your paycheque is deposited each pay period to remove the temptation to spend it. From there, you can set up automatic investments to put the money out of sight and out of mind. Some financial institutions even allow you to request that these transfers increase in value over time automatically. This allows you to make financial decisions your future self will benefit from without having to give anything up today.

Celebrate the Wins

You can also give yourself small rewards along the way to make sure you're satisfying your need for immediate gratification. Celebrations, like going for a nice dinner every few months if you stick to your plan, bring a nice balance. Another approach is to break your goals into smaller chunks that you can celebrate more regularly. A retirement plan doesn't need to be a thirty-year grind without milestones. Reaching $1,000, $20,000 or $100,000 are significant achievements in and of themselves.

Stick to Your Plan

There's a long list of biases you can mitigate with practice. For instance, people don't like to lose. This shows up in a hesitation to invest due to a fear of losing money. It can also lead to the unfortunate situation that investors sell when the market is down, out of fear of losing more. We all overreact to the potential and reality of losing money. Therefore, to avoid making emotionally driven shortcut decisions, you should stick to the plan you set out. If this is to invest for twenty years, then avoid selling when markets drop. This allows your investments the chance to recover and continue to grow toward your goal. In addition to automating your savings, it's important to automate your investment approach. Actively managing your investments can be emotionally draining. It also relies heavily on your subconscious mind, leaving you open to errors.

Motivation

An important aspect of setting aside savings is to remind yourself of the progress you're making. You can keep track of balances to watch your wealth build over time, or you can review your long-term goals to remind yourself of what it's all for. By reminding yourself of the final goal, you'll make the future benefit of your work more real. Your goal may be to travel around the world or put your child through post-secondary education. Either way, it's important to look past the dollars and cents to what it all really means.

Personal finance is a subject that spans the entirety of your life. As such, it's not something you can work at for a few months and then stop. Your regular savings will provide for you well into the future, which is why persistence is so important. Regular reminders of the goals you've reached and progress you've made will help to keep you in the right state of mind.

Final Thoughts

The best way to remove the barriers of behavioural biases is automation. The less day-to-day involvement you have, the less opportunity there is for your subconscious mind to hijack your plans. Saving for the future is critical to ensure your standard of living doesn't decrease over time. After all, though your subconscious mind doesn't think a cookie next week is all that great, when it's finally in your mouth, your taste buds will thank you.

Key Takeaways

- Your subconscious mind takes shortcuts to make decision-making easier.
- Mental shortcuts can lead to errors called biases that make managing your money more challenging.
- Automating your saving and investing is the best way to protect you from your subconscious mind.

Chapter 19

Further Research

Before diving into further research, let's discuss two important concepts: conflicts of interest and the intended audience. Providing information about personal finance is a very popular pastime or job for many people. Their research, opinions and recommendations are readily available for your consideration. While many are well-intentioned, there are some who hope to personally benefit from the information they present. Watching for conflicts of interest will help you avoid acting on information that's not in your best interest.

Detecting Conflicts of Interest

Conflicts of interest occur when the author or someone they know benefits if people follow the advice provided. For example, a forum member could recommend an investment they own, hoping you'll invest and increase the price. Or, a blogger could recommend a product only because they get compensated if you sign up. To know if a conflict of interest is possible, it's important to understand who the author is. Some individuals in the financial industry are obligated to disclose conflicts of interest, while others aren't. If you can't rule out the possibility, it's best to err on the side of safety and look for multiple opinions.

The Intended Audience

The second point to be aware of when researching new ideas is the intended audience of the material. There are many differences between the financial situation of any two people. For instance, some people fear risk more than others. Resources, like articles and books, are created for an intended audience to whom the concepts apply. For example, in Chapter 6, we covered two possible ways to pay off debt. You can pay the smallest balance first, or you can pay the highest interest rate first.

An article titled "Pay Off Your Debt in Order of Smallest to Largest Balances" may not be the best approach for everyone. This is an approach for those who have trouble finding the desire to pay off debt. With this method, you can see real results by eliminating small debts and moving on to the next one. However, as we mentioned before, you could also pay down your debts based on the highest interest rate. Before applying the newest investment trend or budgeting approach, see if it's intended for someone in your situation.

Resources Available

Now that you're ready to critically learn from resources, let's discuss the options. There's a wide assortment of books, websites, blogs, forums and videos that cover personal finance topics. We've talked about several investments for your money that offer different returns. One of the best returns you'll find is spending time and money learning more about financial products and ideas.

Books About Personal Finance

Books are a common source of additional learning because they're convenient, structured and comprehensive. Working through books will provide new ways of thinking, alternate opinions and additional examples. You may come across a concept not seen before, which could better match your situation, or you may read new views on topics you've already seen, which help solidify your understanding. It's often possible to present very convincing arguments for both sides of a decision. If you're only seeing one side of the picture, you may be missing an important trade-off. You can find top-rated books online for topics, like paying off debt, earning more money, investing or preparing for retirement. It's important to balance reading the classics that have stood the test of time while looking for new takes on each topic.

Digital Resources

With an ever-increasing number of online resources, given enough time and effort, you can learn just about anything. Personal finance websites grow in numbers by the day. The best part is that most of them have target audiences, allowing you to find a tailored site just for you. By searching descriptions of your current situation, you'll come across multiple websites for consideration. Statements like "recent graduate with questions about debt payments" will provide articles that point you in the right direction. Personal finance blogs are common because it's a topic that applies to nearly everyone. Finding a blogger with common goals will help you get great ideas that seem like they were written just for you. Visiting forums is helpful to receive summarized articles or discussions on a wide range of questions.

Another great way to learn is through video. The aid of visual cues and audio explanation can offer a more enjoyable way to learn. Topics range from the simplest of terminology all the way to complex financial situations. These videos can be used as a supplement to any existing plan of research and offer a unique experience.

Government Resources

Several of the accessories we covered throughout part II were sponsored by the Government of Canada. The TFSA, RRSP and RESP all provide incentives to save for various goals. Rules for these accounts are provided and enforced by the Canada Revenue Agency (CRA). Occasionally, these rules change, and when this happens, the Government of Canada updates its website. The CRA also provides details about your contribution room and tax records through its online system called My Account. For instance, you can find the amount of contribution room you have through this login under a section called "RRSP and TFSA". To the best of my ability the examples in this book illustrating government-sponsored programs used numbers that were current at the time of publishing. It's important to check the Government of Canada's website for the most up-to-date information.

The Ontario Securities Commission (OSC) is a regulatory body that protects investors in Canada. They also created a website called *Get Smarter About Money* that offers:

- Articles on a wide range of personal finance topics
- Calculators for mortgages, debt repayment, investing and more
- Worksheets for budgeting
- Tools, including quizzes and ideas for life events

These resources are excellent because they avoid much of the risk we noted earlier in this chapter. Topics are presented without a conflict of interest, since their mandate is to protect you, the reader. The information is also presented in an unbiased way, limiting the risk of acting on information not intended for you.

Final Thoughts

Continuing to improve your financial literacy will allow you to take advantage of opportunities today and in the future. You can combine the resources we've discussed in many ways. You may read about a new idea in a book or article. If there are unfamiliar terms, you can watch a video to learn more. And if you have remaining questions, you can visit a blog or forum to get answers. Along the way, remember to explore both sides of the trade-off decision and look for multiple opinions before moving ahead.

Key Takeaways

- Understand potential conflicts of interest and the intended audience before acting on information.
- Earn the highest returns available by investing in your financial knowledge.
- Explore multiple opinions and take advantage of different modes of learning to retain new information.

Chapter 20

Organization and Practice

A financial plan includes a budget, different accounts, multiple investments and more. These all require organization and occasional monitoring to confirm you're on track. Therefore, there's a need for a central point of reference to manage your finances and ensure you're not missing anything.

To do this, you can use a combination of websites, apps or software. A common approach is to use a website that collects all your account information from your different online profiles. It then presents your whole financial picture and tracks your progress over time. You can set up a budget and monitor your spending through one of several popular apps. Future goals can be listed in a word document, and you can plan how much you'll need for each in a spreadsheet. Find a system that's simple to follow, and experiment with different tools over time to see what works best for you.

Simulations in Place of Practice

A common way to learn is through experience. You can try something new and see what works, then ensure that past mistakes don't repeat themselves. However, the opportunity to practice getting a mortgage isn't always an option. As a result, it can be helpful to go through simulations ahead of time to see what different choices may lead to. Simulations include making calculations for different scenarios and seeing what would happen. For instance, you can calculate how much you can afford to pay each month toward a mortgage if you or your partner lost your job. You could also see how much your mortgage payment would increase if interest rates went up. By looking at different calculations, you can make an informed decision and minimize the chance you're caught off guard.

You'll also benefit from seeing how much you need to save each month for retirement given different scenarios. We'll cover this in the Appendix when we discuss the question of how much to save for retirement. Without running multiple calculations, you may over or underestimate the amount of money needed. And in the case of retirement savings, there's no going back for a second chance.

To help, there are calculators online from sites like the OSC's *Get Smarter About Money*. These calculators cover topics like the growth of savings over time, mortgage affordability and insurance requirements. You can compare the expenses of owning a home to the costs of renting without having to do either. By changing the assumptions for important inputs, you'll see a range of scenarios that may take place and the impact each would have on your financial plan.

Key Takeaways

- Find a set of websites, apps or software to help track your progress and spending over time.
- Use calculators to see what the future could hold and prepare for different outcomes.

Chapter 21

Helping Others

A great way to see if you truly understand something is to try and teach it to someone else. Explaining material to others allows you to go over the key points in your head and internalize them. If your teaching is successful, then you can rest assured that you've truly grasped the information gathered.

Whether it's a new budget tracking app or an ETF with lower fees, explain the concept and benefits to someone else. Then, gauge your understanding by how well they can follow along. Many financial topics seem straightforward at first glance. But when you break them down into the steps involved, you realize how many rules or differing interpretations there are. By thinking through what's most relevant for your explanation, it will help you remember what matters most.

Sharing what you know with those around you also allows them the opportunity to return the favour. If you explain the benefits of a TFSA to a friend, they may return the favour later by suggesting a new investment option. You never know the value that could be added to someone's life by helping them with a financial topic. As more people around you become comfortable with personal finance, it can become a helpful, thought-provoking and enjoyable field of conversation.

The success of a community doesn't rest on any one person. The financial success of a community or, more widely a country, relies on the achievements of all its citizens. The more informed, capable and motivated people are the more successful we'll be as a nation. As a result, you share some of your fate with your neighbours and fellow citizens. Even if you're prepared for retirement, if others need financial support, it places higher requirements on your savings. Therefore, your investment in the future should be made not only into your savings account but into helping those around you to better understand and prepare for their own financial future.

Key Takeaways

- You can have a major impact on others by helping them learn about personal finance topics.
- While your financial plan may relate to you and your family, it's impacted by Canada's success as well.

Closing Remarks

You've now seen that the fundamentals of personal finance are as simple as building a snowman.

- Part I covered saving and investing, showing that the steps involved are no different than rolling a snowball after a fresh snowfall.
- Part II discussed additional tools and examples that can be added to your plan like accessories are added to a snowman.
- Part III explained the resources that can help you along the way to reduce the workload and share the benefits with those around you.

We've mentioned that everyone's financial situation is different. You may be comfortable for now with only adding concepts from Chapter 1, or this book could be one of several on a path to mastering your finances. Either way, start first where you're comfortable and expand with time. Like budgeting, financial planning is often tossed aside because it's thought to be too challenging or life-altering. This is because to implement a plan you most likely need to change habits you've been following for most of your life.

If you take on too much at once, the chance of success decreases. It becomes too hard to follow all these new rules and considerations. Just as with adjusting other habits, it's hard to change everything all at once. Instead, you can gradually change the habit over time little by little. Following even the simplest of financial plans will leave you better off than having no plan at all. As your habits shift and you get used to the changes, you can improve the plan and continue to better your financial situation.

With the knowledge collected throughout this book, your financial future is looking increasingly bright. As you continue to expand your knowledge and comfort level with personal finance, I ask that you share it with those around you. The concepts of personal finance can seem daunting, but as we've now seen through this book, they don't have to be. I ask that you look for opportunities to acknowledge the angst many of us initially feel, and point people in the right direction to learn more. Perhaps it's a book you found helpful or a website that may offer some assistance. It's time the subject of personal finance was made accessible for everyone's benefit. Because as we've now seen, if you can build a snowman, you can manage your money with confidence.

Acknowledgments

Writing a book, as I've read from others and now experienced myself, is never a solo task. Critical to writing this book were the motivation and support provided by my family, friends, colleagues and partner.

The initial motivation came from that conversation nearly a decade ago with my brother David and close friend Sumeet. Thank you both for the out of the box conversations that started the long list of analogies included in this book. Along the way friends and colleagues were keen to chat about the content and experience of writing a book. Thank you all for your feedback, ideas and for at least feigning excitement—your interest kept me energized.

I couldn't have asked for more supportive parents. I can recall sending drafts to my father's email faster than he could possibly have read through the previous version. Thank you, mom and dad, for always supporting your boys in all that we do, our achievements are more yours than ours. My older brother Chris was first to purchase the book. Thank you for reading and offering helpful feedback.

Providing me with both motivation and support was my amazing partner Anna. Thank you for your thoughtful gift in printing an early draft. Your encouragement that this book could help others kept me going throughout it all. Thank you for reading through early drafts, providing feedback and whiteboarding with me.

I hope you found this book informative and enjoyable. If you have questions, feedback or topics you'd like to learn more about please email me at steven@snowmansguide.com. While I won't be able to provide advice, I'll be happy to offer explanations and resources I've found helpful in the past. You can also follow me over at www.snowmansguide.com and on Twitter @snowmans_guide.

If you know others who could benefit from the tools and mindsets we've discussed, your referral means everything. If you're comfortable sharing a review on Amazon or Goodreads, I'd love to hear what you enjoyed and anything that can be improved.

If you'd like multiple copies to share with employees, students, clients, club members or otherwise, please connect with me directly for a discount.

Appendix

Next Steps

Setting aside a portion of your money as it's earned is the first step to reaching any financial goal. There's no one-size-fits-all plan for what to do with your money, but the following checklist provides a common set of options. While the order of importance isn't set in stone, you'll be better off with each line you check off. You can start building habits by splitting your money between multiple lines. Or you can remain focused on a single line and check them off one by one. Start where it makes the most sense for you and begin progressing to your financial goals.

To Do	Baseline	Reference
❏ Pay off high-interest debt (e.g., credit card)	>10% interest	Chapter 7
❏ Enroll for any plans with employer contributions	Maximize matching	Chapter 11
❏ Create a rainy day fund for unexpected expenses	Three to six months	Chapter 5
❏ Pay off medium-interest debt (e.g., student loans)	5% to 10% interest	Chapter 7
❏ Set up a registered account depending on your situation (e.g., TFSA, RRSP, RESP)	Contribution limit	Chapters 9, 10 and 16
❏ Pay off low-interest debt (e.g., mortgage)	<5% interest	Chapter 7
❏ Set up a traditional non-registered account	Remaining savings	Chapter 10

While you're working on the above steps, you can also progress through the following items to enhance your financial plan.

To Do	Reference
❏ Set up a budget and track your spending	Chapter 6
❏ Purchase appropriate insurance coverage for your needs	Chapter 8
❏ Create a will as your situation requires it	Chapter 8
❏ Identify a list of goals (e.g., retirement, down payment)	Chapter 5
❏ Determine your desired risk level for each goal	Chapter 4
❏ Decide on a diversified investment option for each goal	Chapter 3
❏ Consolidate your account data to monitor your progress	Chapter 20

Appendix

How to Start Investing

The opportunity to invest your money and earn income while you sleep is hard to pass up. Before we proceed with how to invest, let's confirm you're working on or have completed other important milestones. These include paying off medium- and high-interest debt, like student loans and credit cards. Setting up an emergency fund with three to six months' expenses so you don't have to sell your investments early. And signing up for any retirement plan with contributions made by your employer. If all of these are complete or underway, congratulations, and let's start putting more of your money to work.

Set a Goal

The first step to investing is to set a goal for your money. This is important for two reasons. The first is it helps you answer the next set of questions around timeframe, risk tolerance and more. The second is that it makes the outcome of your savings more real and motivating. Whether it's to travel next summer or simply to grow a second source of income, it's helpful to have a goal. Common goals include:

- ☐ a down payment or renovation
- ☐ a sabbatical or attending school
- ☐ retirement
- ☐ starting a business
- ☐ or peace of mind that you'll have a head start when something comes up

Set a Timeline

The second step is to decide when you'll need the money. As we've mentioned throughout the book, high-risk investments like stocks are unpredictable. If you need the money in a year or two, your investment options are different than saving for something ten years off. As a result, try to determine which range your goal falls into.

❏ Short-term	❏ Medium-term	❏ Long-term
less than 2 years	3 to 6 years	7 or more years

Decide Your Risk Level

The third step is to decide your risk level. In addition to knowing when you need your money, it's also important to consider several other factors. These include:

- how comfortable you are with risk
- how much, if any, you can afford to lose

If you're uncomfortable with risk and would lose sleep if your investments declined in value, you may want a safer investment. As you learn more about investing and experience it, you may become more comfortable with risk. If you can't afford to lose money because your timing and amount needed are fixed, you may want a safer investment. After confirming your time horizon, you can shift your risk level to the left based on your flexibility and comfort with risk.

Short-term	Medium-term	Long-term
less than 2 years	3 to 6 years	7 or more years

If your goal is less flexible or you're less comfortable with uncertainty, shift down your risk level

◀ − − − − − − − − − − ◀ − − − − − − − − − −

❏ Low risk	❏ Medium risk	❏ High risk

Decide Your Involvement

The fourth step is to decide how involved you want to be in the investment process. If the previous step has you uncertain which risk level is right for you, it may be worth receiving guidance from an expert. If you're confident so far, you may be able to take a more hands-on approach. There are ways to invest that fall all along the spectrum from hands-off to hands-on.

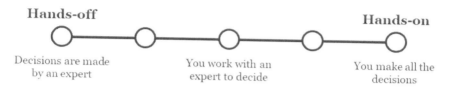

Hands-off   **Hands-on**

Decisions are made by an expert   You work with an expert to decide   You make all the decisions

Pick a Product

The fifth step is to pick one of the many products available in Canada. A short list of options we've discussed in this book include:

- A high-interest savings account (HISA) opened directly with a bank or digital provider
- A brokerage account to buy a wide list of investments online yourself
- A professional advisor to receive financial planning support in addition to recommended investments

Because there are so many options, the first four steps are critical to help you narrow them down. To do this, the following chart helps categorize options by the level of risk and your involvement. The bolded words are the relationship you set up, and the normal font words are the types of investments you can choose. In the case of an expert, they'd have access to a wide range of investments and would work with you to find the right fit.

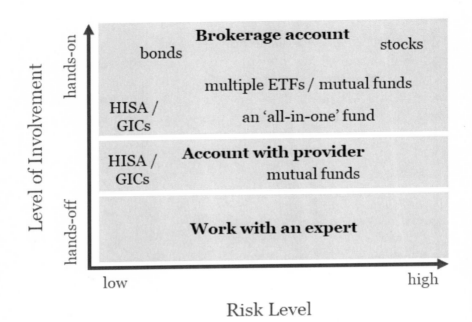

The three main relationships you can establish are:

1. Opening a brokerage account and then investing in a wide range of options yourself
   - As we mentioned in Chapter 14, you can open a brokerage account through several online providers and most banks.
2. Opening an individual investment directly with the provider. Examples include opening a HISA or GIC, or buying a mutual fund directly
   - Opening a HISA or GIC directly from the financial institution may provide a higher return than buying them in a brokerage account. You can also purchase mutual funds with low fees and minimums online.
3. Finding an expert, either in person or online, to invest your money for you
   - Experts go by many names, including financial advisor, investment advisor and robo-advisor. It's important to get the right value for your fees and to ensure they're looking out for your best interests.

All three options allow you to invest in low-, medium- or high-risk investments. With a low-risk level, you're likely best opening a HISA or GIC. You can do this through a bank or digital provider directly, in a brokerage account or through an expert. If your risk level is medium or high, you can work with an expert in person or online to invest your money. You could also open an account directly with a mutual fund provider online. Or you could open a brokerage account and manage your investments yourself.

Within a brokerage account, you have different options depending on your level of involvement. You could manage stocks and bonds yourself, you could buy several ETFs or mutual funds or you could buy a single all-in-one fund. All-in-one—or one ticket— funds are new and help minimize your fees if you're comfortable being a bit hands-on. A single ETF invests your money into a diversified portfolio and rebalances it for you, all based on your selected risk level.

Typically, the more hands-off you are, the more you'll pay in fees. As we've mentioned, this may include fees charged by funds or paid to your advisor. In Chapter 14, we showed that an additional 1.25% in annual fees can lower the amount you have for your goal by 30%. If you take on a bit more of the work and use a brokerage account to buy an all-in-one fund, you'll lower your fees. However, if you receive value for the fees you pay, there's no concern. Having peace of mind, guidance on where and how to invest your money and someone to coach you along the way is valuable.

If you're not sure which is right, you can always start with a no minimum hands-off approach and go from there. This could include meeting with an expert in person. Or, if you prefer to invest online and don't need to meet in person, you can use a new option called a robo-advisor. Fees for a robo-advisor are lower than most hands-off options. Robo-advisors allow you to see the investment process and learn along the way. As you become more comfortable with investing and the options available, you may gradually become more hands-on. This helps lower your fees and puts more of your money toward your goals.

Open an Account

The sixth step is to open an account. At this stage, you've decided your goal, timeline, risk level, level of involvement and product to open. It's now time to decide which specific company to use and what type of account to open. The most common way to choose a company is to use an online comparison guide that looks at fees, usability and more. Keep in mind our topic of conflicts of interest, as some guides receive compensation if you open an account they recommend. Therefore, you'll also want to consider ratings from existing clients.

If you're taking a hands-off approach and are working with an expert, this next part is less relevant. If you're taking a hands-on approach, you'll need to decide which type of account to open. We've already discussed the most common types of accounts. These include the TFSA, RRSP, non-registered account and RESP.

❑ TFSA	❑ RRSP	❑ Non-registered	❑ Other
• Tax-free growth • Withdraw anytime	• Reduce income taxes owed	• Taxed on growth • No limit	• For specific goals and situations

If you're saving for retirement, you'll need to decide between a TFSA or RRSP. We discussed this in depth in Chapter 10 and found that it primarily depends on your income. If you're looking to get started and aren't certain which is right, you can open a TFSA and switch to an RRSP later if needed.

If you're saving for shorter-term goals, a TFSA is almost always the right choice. If you've maxed out your contribution limit, then saving in a non-registered account may make sense. If you're saving for a child's education, you're likely best opening an RESP account. Once you've decided on the company and account type, you can open most accounts online. You'll likely need personal information, like your Social Insurance Number (SIN) and some bank information.

Deposit Your Money

The seventh and final step is to deposit your money. This can include up-front deposits that you may have already saved and ongoing deposits. For up-front deposits, there are two ways you can proceed. Depending on the amount of money and type of investment, you could deposit everything at once. If your investment is low risk, like a savings account or GIC, you're likely best doing it all at once. If, however, you have a large amount to invest and are choosing a medium- or high-risk investment, you could deposit gradually. This approach lowers the chance that you'll invest everything and lose a large portion the following week. You could invest your money monthly in pre-set amounts over six to twelve months to lower the chance of regret.

For ongoing deposits, as we've discussed throughout the book, it's best to do this automatically. You can set up a transfer to your investment account that automatically happens every paycheque. Once your money is in the account, some products invest automatically. If your account is directly with a mutual fund provider or a robo-advisor, your money is invested shortly after deposit. If you're investing in a brokerage account, you may need to invest your new deposit yourself. Some providers allow you to automate this process online or by filling out a form.

There are two ways you can decide how much money to transfer to your account. These are based on:

1. How much you have available
    - If you've built your budget and are saving a set amount each month, you can apply all or part to your new account.
2. How much you'll need
    - You can calculate how much you'll need for your goal and work backwards to see how much to set aside.

With the first approach, you can decide how many goals you have and how important or time-sensitive each one is. Based on this, you'll determine how much of your savings to assign to the account. In the second case, you'll need to decide how much you need. This may be a simple answer if you're saving for a vacation or house and know the amount you want to withdraw. Then, it's a matter of dividing that amount by the number of deposits. A more complicated goal like retirement can be harder to determine. As a result, we'll address this question in further detail shortly.

Final Thoughts

We've now covered the seven steps to start investing. In addition, it's important to remember the material we've discussed throughout this book. Some topics that are most relevant include:

- The power of compound growth and the importance of investing in higher return options if your risk level allows it
- Diversifying your investments to minimize risk of losses
- Sticking to your plan and ignoring the noise of the ups and downs of the market

If you're just starting off, opening a TFSA with an online robo-advisor is a simple way to take advantage of most of the benefits mentioned in this book. If you'd like to speak with an expert in person or feel comfortable taking a hands-on approach, there are lots of great choices available. It's important not to give up due to confusion or uncertainty of what's best. Often, we spend much of our time discussing the minor benefits of one option over another. We forget that they all offer a great way to put your money to work and take full control of your financial future.

Key Takeaways

- Seven simple steps will allow you to pick the right investment approach for your needs.
- Don't delay starting because you want to find the perfect approach. Start early and learn as you go.
- Ensure you're getting value for the fees you pay, otherwise switch providers or be more hands-on.

Appendix

How Much to Save for Retirement

A rule of thumb for retirement savings is to set aside 10% of your income. However, this depends on a long list of inputs, including:

- Your current age
- Any existing savings
- When you hope to retire
- Your comfort level with higher-risk investments

For instance, if you plan to retire at sixty-five, you'll need to save less of your income than if you want to retire at fifty. While the answer to how much you need to save varies, it will help to see a base case, and then, we can continue from there.

A Sample Retirement Savings Plan

We'll start with a list of assumptions for Olivia, a twenty-five-year-old living in Calgary.

- Twenty-five years old
- No existing retirement savings
- Planned retirement age of sixty-five
- Comfortable with riskier investments

With these assumptions, and a few others, we can determine how much Olivia needs to set aside each year for retirement.

First, we need to forecast how much Olivia will earn over her career to see what saving 10% would lead to. Olivia expects to increase her income by 4% a year for the next ten years as she takes online courses and expands her skillset. For the remainder of her career, she expects her salary to increase with inflation at 2%.

Exhibit 47 – Between age twenty-five and sixty-five, Olivia's income increases from $40,000 to $105,000.

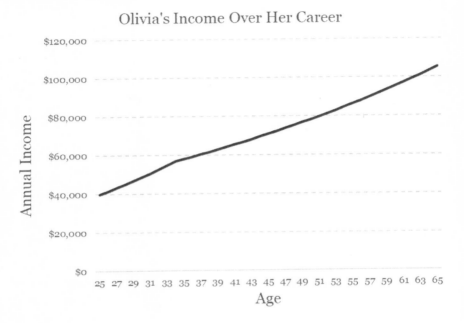

Olivia's Income Over Her Career

Saving 10%

If Olivia sets aside 10% of her income each year, she'd deposit a total of $294,100 to her savings account before retirement. On top of what she sets aside, Olivia could invest her savings to help them grow. Olivia has a long timeframe and is comfortable with riskier investments. Therefore, we'll assume she starts with mostly high-risk investments before gradually shifting to more low-risk investments.

Exhibit 48 – By investing her money, Olivia could accumulate $790,200 for retirement. She begins earning an average annual growth of 7%, which gradually falls to 4% as she shifts to lower-risk investments.

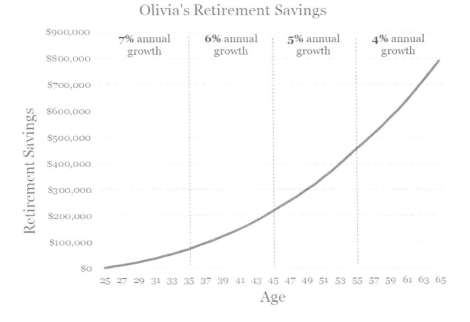

Savings Compared to Income

In addition to the rule of thumb of saving 10%, you can also look at your total savings compared to your current income. In Olivia's case, we can divide her savings by her income at each age to see how much she's accumulated.

Exhibit 49 – The following table shows how many years of income Olivia has in savings from age twenty-five to sixty-five.

Age	Income	Savings	[x] Times Her Income Saved
25	$40,000	$4,000	0.1
30	$48,666	$31,388	0.6
35	$58,071	$75,273	1.3
40	$64,115	$135,404	2.1
45	$70,788	$219,482	3.1
50	$78,156	$321,567	4.1
55	$86,291	$456,169	5.3
60	$95,272	$604,540	6.3
65	$105,188	$790,213	7.5

Exhibit 50 – Olivia's case can be simplified to the following table to use as a general benchmark.

Age	30	35	40	45	50	55	60	65
[x] Times Your Income Saved	1	1.5	2	3	4	5	6	8

Why Save for Retirement

It's important to save for retirement so you don't need to dramatically change your lifestyle when you stop working. For instance, if you spend $60,000 a year and leave your job without savings, you'll need to cut back significantly. You may receive some income from government programs. These include the Canada Pension Plan (CPP) and Old Age Security (OAS) for most Canadians. Low-income individuals may also receive the Guaranteed Income Supplement (GIS). However, this income is rarely enough to support you on its own. As a result, you'll need savings when you retire so you can continue spending at a suitable level. Travelling, visiting family and maintaining your home likely all require the use of existing savings.

To demonstrate how this works, we'll continue with Olivia's situation. As we saw above, with 10% savings, Olivia reaches a total of $790,200 before retiring. Once she retires, she'll need to use these savings and government pension income to cover her expenses. Since some of her money is going toward savings and costs for her job, she expects her expenses to decline once she retires. For instance, she'll no longer need to save for retirement or pay to commute to work. Through lowered costs and government pensions, Olivia expects she'll need $43,000 from her own savings the first year. For simplicity, we'll assume this continues through retirement, increasing each year with inflation.

Exhibit 51 – If Olivia earns 3.5% growth on her savings during retirement, she'd run out of savings at the age of eighty-seven.

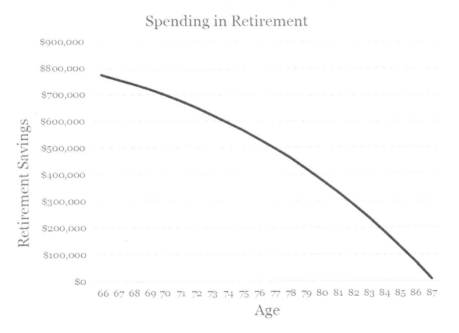

Exhibit 52 – Combining the working and retirement periods shows how savings are used to provide a consistent lifestyle over time.

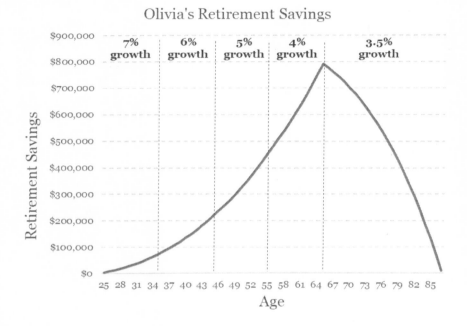

Olivia's Retirement Savings

Other Considerations

Olivia's case is a simple view that relies on assumptions that may not come true. If her investment returns are lower than planned, she could run out of money earlier. She may also want to consider other factors, including:

- How her home value can be used in retirement
- Her life expectancy
- How much she could lower her spending if required

To give a sense of how these and other factors could impact your retirement plan, let's review several cases.

Exhibit 53 – If Olivia earns a lower rate of return on her investments, she could run out of savings at the age of eighty.

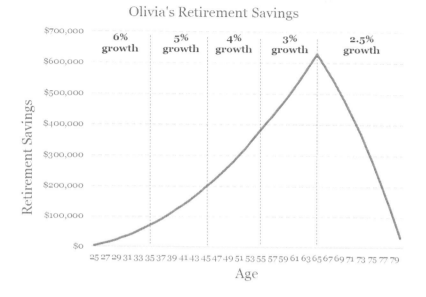

Exhibit 54 – If she expects to live to ninety-two, she'd need to save 12% of her income instead of 10%.

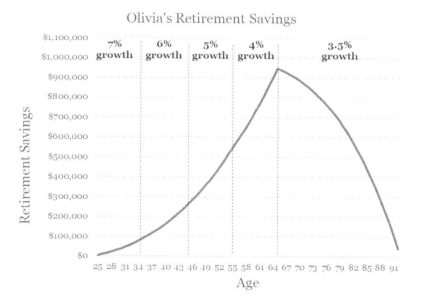

Final Thoughts

While the rule of thumb to save 10% of your income for retirement is a great start, we've seen that each case is unique. As we mentioned in Chapter 6, saving for the future allows you to maintain your standard of living over your lifetime. If you're able to, saving earlier will provide a great head start. As we saw in Chapter 2 with Daniel and Craig, compound returns are the most useful tool to helping you reach your goal. If you're starting later than you'd have liked, that's not a problem, you're now further ahead than you were yesterday. If your employer offers a retirement plan with matching contributions, sign up as soon as you can. Otherwise, open a TFSA or RRSP and start making regular, automatic deposits. You'll be amazed how quickly steady contributions add up.

Key Takeaways

- Save 10% of your income for retirement if you're starting early and slightly more if you've waited to start.
- Aim to have twice your income in savings by forty and eight times your income by sixty-five.
- Once you know when you want to retire and what it'll involve, you can adjust these amounts accordingly.

Manufactured by Amazon.ca
Acheson, AB